A SILK RIBBON Album

Jenifer Buechel

Martingale
& COMPANY

Bothell, Washington

Dedication

For Marion Nath, a wonderful neighbor, friend, and substitute mom.
Thank you for all your support, encouragement, and advice …
whether I needed it or not. You have taught me more than you know.

Acknowledgments

My thanks to:

All my students, who always inspire me with their enthusiasm and desire to learn.

Nancy Howard and her stitching group at the Knittin' Kitten: Marcia de Rosas, Edith Kindred, Nancy Maher, Ellen O'Sullivan, Mary Shea, and Mary Anne Wedlock. Your accomplishments speak for themselves.

Robin Giehll for letting me borrow her talents for this book.

Janet Wigg for jumping in to help, and for always threatening to become a "groupie."

Mary Ann Lipinski—you have become a wonderful inspiration. You have an incredible talent for making my quilt designs look stunning.

Jill Dodin for a great job quilting.

Ardeth Laake—you are my very special inspiration both in quilting and in life.

Sue Gilbert, my incredible Appliqué Academy friend—your friendship and support (as close as a phone call away) have become an important part of my life.

Martingale and Company for the opportunity to write another book, especially Melissa Lowe, who always had time to listen. I'm going to miss you, Melissa.

The family I love—Ron, Heather, and Ryan—for your support while this book took over my life (even though none of you would stitch for me).

And as always, thanks to my best friend and sister, Joy Mays. You are truly one of the lights of my life. Love ya.

MISSION STATEMENT

We are dedicated to providing quality products and service by working together to inspire creativity and to enrich the lives we touch.

Library of Congress Cataloging-in-Publication Data
Buechel, Jenifer
    A silk-ribbon album : more than 30 miniature quilt blocks / Jenifer Buechel.
       p. cm.
    Includes bibliographical references and index.
    ISBN 1-56477-229-2
    1. Patchwork—Patterns. 2. Quilting—Patterns. 3. Silk ribbon embroidery. 4. Album quilts. 5. Miniature quilts. I. Title.
TT835.B784 1998
746.46'041—dc21
                           98-20265
                               CIP

Credits

President: Nancy J. Martin
Publisher/CEO: Daniel J. Martin
Associate Publisher: Jane Hamada
Editorial Director: Mary Green
Technical Editor: Cindy Brick
Production Manager: Cheryl Stevenson
Cover Designer: Jim Gerlitz
Text Designer: Kay Green
Illustrator: Laurel Strand
Photographer: Brent Kane

A Silk-Ribbon Album
© 1998 by Jenifer Buechel

Martingale
& C O M P A N Y

Martingale & Company
PO Box 118
Bothell, WA 98041-0118 USA

Printed in Hong Kong
03 02 01 00 99 98   6 5 4 3 2 1

CONTENTS

INTRODUCTION

As I was designing quilt blocks for my first book, *Miniature Baltimore Album Quilts*, I realized I had more patterns than could fit into just one volume. The majority of these patterns were for what I call "Red and Green" blocks. They were based on traditional motifs and were usually appliquéd in red and green fabrics.

After showing some of the blocks to students and shop owners, I decided to make a Christmas quilt. I used holly in place of the traditional rounded leaves, then added snowflake background fabric—I think I got a little carried away.

Since I wanted to use this quilt as a class project, I scoured the embroidery books on my shelves, looking for different stitches that would translate well into silk-ribbon embroidery. You will find a few of these new stitches here, along with the more traditional stitches. I've also included stitch combinations for creating layered ribbon flowers.

One of the objectives of this book is to allow you not only to make your quilt, but also to participate in its design and layout. The blocks, medallion settings, and border patterns can be mixed and matched, so you can create a unique and interesting quilt that shows your personality. Above all else, enjoy the process and have fun.

GETTING STARTED

Please read all the instructions before you begin. There are tips and suggestions throughout the book that will make creating your miniature quilt easier.

To begin, you need to decide how many blocks you want in your quilt and what kind of setting you want to use. Thirty-two block patterns (pages 58–91) and a medallion center with two different corner variations (page 55) are included in this book. You can choose holly sprigs for a festive holiday look or rounded leaves for a more traditional style.

If you like, you can frame your blocks and medallion with one of two appliqué patterns (pages 104–5). And for the finishing touch, there are a variety of border designs (pages 106–8) to choose from.

After you have determined how many blocks you want and the setting you will use, gather the supplies and materials needed for one block. Follow the step-by-step instructions for constructing (page 13) and embroidering (page 16) the blocks, then assemble and finish your quilt (pages 92–103).

The following pages cover just some of the options for making your own miniature. Have fun and be creative!

Designing Your Quilt

A number of layout options are shown in this book—look through the photo gallery on pages 17–40 for inspiration. The layout you choose will determine the size of your blocks and the yardage you'll need.

Because I usually design quilts on my computer, I can draw blocks and manipulate the layout onscreen until I am happy with the results. This method makes it easy for me to visualize the finished quilt from the start.

You don't need a computer to play with block designs and settings, though. Since these blocks are small, all you need is paper. Just trace or photocopy block designs onto paper, then trim the blocks to finished size. Experiment with different layouts, using the paper mockups, before you cut any fabrics. Label each block you decide to use with a number, so you can identify your block placement quickly. Use the final mockup to help calculate yardage for your quilt. For information on choosing fabrics, see pages 8–9.

Keep the following hints in mind as you choose your blocks and determine your layout:

❋ For design ideas, review the quilts on pages 17–24, or look at Red and Green quilts in other books. (See the "Bibliography" on page 110 for help.)

❋ Study the way other quilters set blocks together. Red and Green quilts are traditionally symmetrical, or balanced. If you have a Basket block in one area of the quilt, the opposite area of the quilt should also have a basket; not necessarily the same one, but a similar motif. Repeat this concept for wreaths, Whig rose blocks, and corner blocks, balancing one half of the quilt with the other. Evenly distribute color as well.

Choosing a Setting

For the following quilt settings, I recommend that you cut fabric squares at least 1½" to 2" larger than your block's finished size. (All the cutting and yardage instructions take this into account.) This extra fabric will allow you to adjust the block size (there may be some shrinkage from stitching) and make sure the pattern is centered on the finished block. To calculate yardage for a setting, refer to "Estimating Yardage and Cutting Blocks" on pages 7–8.

STRAIGHT SETTINGS

The straight-set quilt is the simplest option; just sew blocks together in rows. The quilt shown on page 17 is an example of this style.

A straight setting allows you to place the medallion block in the center of the quilt, arrange 12 or 32 blocks around it, then add a border.

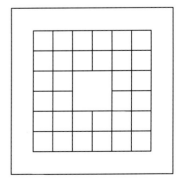

Or, you could eliminate the medallion, set together any number of blocks, and finish with a border.

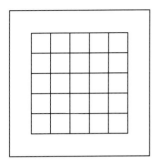

For a straight setting, you need:

Blocks: A 6" square of background fabric for each block in your quilt (finished size is 4").

Medallion: A 10" square of background fabric (finished size is 8").

Borders: Four 5"-wide strips, cut as long as your finished quilt plus 8".

SASHING

You may want to add traditional sashing between each block of a straight-set quilt. Sashing separates the blocks into distinct entities. For this option, the size of the background square is the same as for a straight setting, but the finished size is different. Refer to "Adding Sashing Strips" on pages 93–94 for finished block sizes and sashing methods.

For blocks set with sashing, you need:

Blocks: A 6" square of background fabric for each block in your quilt. (Finished size is determined by the sashing method.)

Medallion: A 10" square of background fabric. (Finished size is determined by the sashing method.)

Borders: Four 5"-wide strips, as long as your finished quilt plus 10".

DIAGONAL SETTINGS

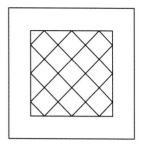

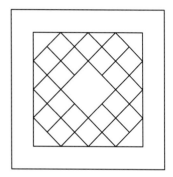

Diagonal settings take a little more planning than straight settings. Although any of the patterns in this book can be set on the diagonal and still fit in the 4" finished block, you may have to rotate the pattern or center it again. For example, Block 11, shown below, would have to be turned on the diagonal to fit inside a finished 4" block.

If you would rather not rotate the block pattern to fit a 4" block, just increase the finished size of all your blocks to accommodate the patterns you want to include.

NOTE
Make sure that your chosen blocks fit in a diagonal setting before you start marking the blocks.

If you want to include a medallion in your diagonal setting, make a paper mockup of your layout. That way, you can determine finished block sizes and the size of the setting triangles you'll need as fillers.

※　※　※

For a diagonal setting, you need:
    Blocks: A 6" square of background fabric for each block in your quilt (finished size is 4").
    Medallion: A 10" square of background fabric (finished size is 8").
    Borders: Four 5"-wide strips, as long as your finished quilt plus 10".
See "Estimating Yardage and Cutting Blocks" on pages 7–8 to figure the yardage you need.

APPLIQUÉD FRAME SETTINGS
Appliqué frames are decorative alternatives to traditional sashing, and they work with both straight and diagonal settings. The following instructions assume you are going to make a straight setting. To adapt diagonally set blocks for appliqué frames, refer to "Assembling Diagonal Settings" on pages 95–96. See "Estimating Yardage and Cutting Blocks" on pages 7–8 to figure the yardage you need.

The Single Frame
The single frame is designed to work with any of the patterns in this book. "Framed for Christmas" on page 18 uses a single frame around each block and the companion border. For a single-frame setting, you need:
    Blocks: A 6½" square each of background and frame fabric for each block in your quilt (finished size is 5½").
    Medallion: A 12" square each of background and frame fabric (finished size is 11").
    Borders (for estimating purposes only; actual length may vary): Four 6½"-wide strips each of the background and frame fabrics, as long as your finished quilt plus 12".

The Double Frame

The double-frame encloses each block in two coordinating fabrics, as in "Memories of Mom" on page 22.

NOTE
Some of the block patterns will not automatically fit into a double-frame design. All of the Basket, Cornucopia, and Wreath designs will work, but others in this collection should be tested for fit before you start. If you want to use block patterns that don't fit comfortably inside the inner circle, you will have to increase the size of both frames, as well as the blocks and border design. Another option is to eliminate the middle frame altogether and use only the outer frame with each block.

❅   ❅   ❅

For a double frame, you need three coordinating fabrics, ranging from light to dark. For this type of setting, you need:

Blocks: A 6½" square each of background and frame fabric for each block in your quilt (finished size is 5½").

Medallion: A 12" square each of background and frame fabric (finished size is 11").

Borders (for estimating purposes only): Four 6½"-wide strips of background fabric and four 6½"-wide strips of frame fabric, as long as your finished quilt plus 12".

Estimating Yardage and Cutting Blocks

BACKGROUND AND FRAME FABRICS

After you have decided on the number of blocks and whether you want to include a medallion, you need to figure yardage for your quilt. All instructions in this book are written for 42"-wide fabric, with measurements based on 40" of usable width for insurance.

Cutting Blocks and a Medallion

Say you want to make the Christmas quilt shown on page 17, with all thirty-two small blocks, the medallion, and the borders. You need a 6" square of fabric for each block and a 10" square for the medallion. You should be able to cut six blocks across a 6" width of your fabric. Cut the medallion from a 10" width; 1¼ yards (which

includes a few extra inches of fabric for insurance) will yield four rows of six blocks each, plus a medallion. Use the leftover fabric to cut eight more blocks, for a total of thirty-two blocks.

Figuring and Cutting Border Strips

Cut the border strips 5" wide (4½" finished size). To figure the strip length, multiply the number of blocks across the quilt by 4" (each block's finished width). There are six blocks in the Christmas quilt example: 6 x 4" = 24". Add 4½" each for the lengthwise and crosswise borders: 9". Add 2" for seam allowances and a little extra for possible mitered corners: 5". Combine these numbers for your needed strip length: 40". Four 5"-wide border strips, each up to 40" long, can be cut widthwise from a 21" length of fabric (⅝ yard).

Generally, you'll cut your quilt's borders, blocks, and medallion from one fabric. For this quilt, 2 yards will be more than ample.

NOTE
The sample quilt is square, so the border strips in this example are all the same length. If your design is rectangular, you'll have two sets of border strips: one for the length and another for the width. Figure them accordingly.

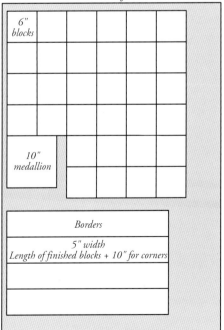

42"-wide fabric

❅   ❅   ❅

Figuring Appliqué Fabrics

Most, if not all, of the appliqué pieces in these quilts could fit on scraps from your collection. Think of it: you could make a new quilt, and make a small dent in your fabric pile in the process!

Many quilters, however, want to make sure they have enough fabric on hand. And since traditional Red and Green quilts often use coordinated fabrics rather than scrappy ones, a selection of fat quarters that fits the color and design pointers in "Appliqué Fabrics" (page 9) should be helpful.

Figuring and Cutting Backing and Binding

A good rule of thumb is to cut backing 4" wider than the quilt top on all sides, to allow for shrinkage during quilting. Since the finished Christmas quilt measures 33" x 33", you'll need a 37" square of fabric (1⅛ yards) for backing.

To estimate the yardage needed to bind the quilt, see "Binding" on pages 102–3.

YARDAGE TIPS

❋ When choosing fabrics for framed layouts, be sure to get identical amounts of the two or three fabrics needed.

❋ Diagonally set quilts use the same layout as straight settings; however, you need to add fabric for setting triangles. When cutting triangles, make sure the long side is on the straight of grain. (See "Assembling and Finishing Your Quilt" on pages 92–103 for help with the diagonal setting.)

❋ If you are backing or binding your quilt with any of the fabrics used in the blocks, medallions, or borders, don't procrastinate. Buy all your fabric at the same time. Otherwise, it may not be there when you need it!

CUTTING YOUR FABRICS

Before you cut your blocks, be sure to prewash your fabric and test it for colorfastness as described under "Fabric" at right. Iron your fabric before cutting.

1. Trim the selvage edges. Following the layout used to determine your yardage, use a rotary cutter, ruler, and cutting mat to cut strips the width of the block and/or medallion you plan to use.

2. Cut the strips into the number of squares needed. If you do not have a rotary cutter, use a marking pencil to draw a grid on the fabric, then cut out the blocks with fabric scissors.

Materials
FABRIC

I recommend using only good quality, tightly woven 100% cotton fabric for your miniature quilt. It is important to prewash fabric in warm water, with or without detergent, to remove the manufacturer's sizing. If you don't remove the sizing, it might prevent the fusible web from bonding tightly with the fabric, and your appliqués could loosen as you embroider them.

Prewashing also lets you see if the fabric is colorfast. Following the wash cycle, check the rinse water for excess dye (colored water). Repeat the rinse cycle twice. If you still see excess dye in the rinse water, don't use that fabric. Fabric that's not colorfast could bleed all over the rest of your quilt. Don't take chances: prewash.

Background Fabric

Antique Red and Green quilts feature white or off-white solid background fabrics. Today we have many more choices. I particularly favor the subtle tone-on-tone prints so popular today. If you want to add a festive spark, a wide assortment of Christmas fabrics, featuring a touch of gold or silver, are often available year-round. As you choose fabric, keep in mind that the color and value of the background will influence the colors and values of the appliqué fabrics, threads, and silk ribbons. The color and value of your background should complement, not compete, with the rest of the quilt.

If you choose a print for your background fabric, I recommend a subtle one: a large-scale print would be out of proportion with the miniature blocks and would detract from the delicacy of your quilt. Also, some fabrics are printed with a heavy ink that sits on top of the fabric. (If you rub the fabric between your fingers, you can feel it.) These fabrics are harder to stitch and can make embroidery more difficult.

While you're choosing a background, it's also a good idea to think about a backing fabric. You may want to use one fabric for the background squares, medallion, borders, and backing. It is better to purchase enough fabric right away than to decide you want it later when it is no longer available.

It usually works best for your backing fabric to be similar in shade to the top of the quilt, or lighter. Otherwise, a dark backing fabric may "shadow" through the front of a light-colored quilt. Test your choices by laying the background fabric on top of the backing fabric to see if it shows through.

To estimate the yardage needed to bind the quilt, see "Binding" on pages 102–3.

Frame Fabric

If you want to accent your blocks with one of the appliquéd frames, you will want to choose the fabric(s) for the frames next. The frame fabric will be the determining factor when you choose colors for appliqué motifs. I recommend a color or print that complements the theme of your quilt. For example, in my Christmas version, shown on page 18, I used a red-and-gold Christmas print for the frame. For the appliqués, I chose reds, a gold, and greens that coordinated with the print. Consider the following suggestions when choosing fabrics:

❊ Choose a small overall print with no obvious repeats. I recommend staying away from diagonals, stripes, large-scale designs, and border prints. When you use these types of fabrics, it takes more time, fabric, and planning to make each block identical. They're also harder to line up correctly when you're assembling your quilt top.

❊ Be dramatic. Select a color or colors that contrast sharply with the background fabric. Let the fabrics used for the appliqué motifs pull everything together.

❊ If you are unsure about any of the fabrics you have selected, make a trial block to help you visualize the finished quilt. It's better to work out your selection before you cut out all the blocks than to decide afterward that you should have made other choices.

Appliqué Fabrics

Red and Green Album quilts traditionally feature a limited color palette. Often there are only one or two shades each of red and green fabrics, plus a gold accent fabric. In this project, you need to consider not only the fabric, but also the ribbons and threads you will use. These embellishments are secondary "fabric" shades that complement your initial fabric choices.

For example, traditional Red and Green Album quilts often use two shades of green throughout, usually for leaves and stems. In your miniature, you can duplicate this look by using a single fabric for the leaves and a coordinating shade of floss and ribbon for the stem and leaf embroidery. Look through the photo gallery on pages 17–40 for color and fabric ideas.

Small-scale prints, or mini-prints, are ideal for the appliqué pieces. Textured and tone-on-tone prints are also wonderful, particularly for leaves. If you are thinking about using a large-scale print, I recommend that you experiment with a block or two before committing to the fabric. You might not be able to cut consistent-looking pieces from a large-scale print.

Since one of the options for your miniature quilt is a Christmas variation, it's hard to resist the temptation to use specialty fabrics, such as lamé and satin. Specialty fabrics need special attention. They may fray, discolor from the heat of the iron, and cause general mayhem. For best results, test the fabric to see if it will fuse to the background fabric. Also, use a pressing cloth and don't include a fabric heavier than cotton.

If you want to use a specialty fabric, stabilize it with a fusible tricot interfacing before you appliqué. This interfacing is available in white and black, and should be coordinated with the fabric color you are using. Follow the manufacturer's instructions for fusing it to the wrong side of the fabric, then use it as you would any other fabric.

FUSIBLE WEB

The embroidery on these blocks is strictly decorative. The appliqué pieces are fused rather than stitched to the background fabric. One yard of lightweight paper-backed fusible web is probably more than enough to make an entire miniature quilt.

NOTE
Don't try to use up old paper-backed fusible web in these blocks. Older paper-backed fusible web doesn't seem to bond well. Because the embroidery on this quilt isn't meant to hold the appliqué in place, the bond between the appliqué and the background fabric is very important.

❊ ❊ ❊

EMBROIDERY FLOSS AND THREAD

Select your floss colors at the same time you choose your fabrics. As a rule, choose a lighter or darker value of the same color used for the appliqué pieces. Remember: the floss almost becomes the secondary fabric, and should be treated as a complementing color. Keep track of dye lot numbers for the flosses and any silk ribbons you choose, in case you need to buy more. (Why not jot the numbers inside the cover of this book? That way, you will always have your notes handy.)

Two strands of embroidery floss or equivalent-weight thread are enough to highlight the appliqué pieces without overwhelming them. Don't feel you have to limit yourself to embroidery floss, though. Experiment with other types of thread. Or try mixing different flosses on one needle.

Embroidery floss: Six-stranded cotton embroidery floss, such as DMC, is readily available and comes in a multitude of colors. Cross-stitchers "strip" the floss (that is, they separate the strands) and thread the number of strands needed onto a needle. Stripping makes the floss easier to control. It also gives you the option of using two colors at the same time, creating the illusion of a new color.

Single-strand cotton floss is also available. This has a matte finish rather than a shiny one. One strand is generally equivalent to two strands of embroidery floss. Single-strand flosses may fray and shred as you stitch; for best results, work with 12"-long pieces.

Metallic threads, blending filaments, and rayon threads: Decorative threads add a delightful sparkle to blocks. Use them alone, or combine them with one strand of embroidery floss. (Make sure the eye of your embroidery needle is large enough to accommodate the threads, though.) Some metallic threads tend to snag on the fabric weave as you embroider. If this happens, switch to a slightly larger embroidery needle (which makes a bigger hole in the fabric), and you will have less trouble. Rayon thread has a tendency to twist and shred as you stitch, so keep your thread length to 12" and wax the thread.

Silk floss and buttonhole twist: While silk threads are not as easy to find as embroidery floss, they can be a real treat to work with. They have an irresistible sheen! Silk buttonhole twist is slightly thicker than two strands of embroidery floss and may be a little more difficult to control, but it is well worth the effort. Remember to keep the thread length to 12". Also, wax your floss or twist with beeswax to limit tangling.

Wool thread: Wool thread, available in a wide range of colors, adds a unique texture and look to appliqué blocks. Like cotton floss, wool thread may fray and shred as you stitch. For best results, work with 12"-long pieces.

SILK RIBBON

Silk-ribbon work is experiencing a popular revival. The softness and drape of ribbon makes it perfect for creating dimensional flowers and leaves. Silk ribbon is usually available at fabric, quilting, and craft stores, as well as through mail-order suppliers. Read the package label and make sure it is 100% silk; it could be synthetic, which is slightly cheaper than the real thing. You can use synthetic silk ribbon, but it may be more difficult to manipulate.

Silk ribbon is available in different widths: 2mm, 4mm, 7mm, 13mm, and wider. The blocks in this book are scaled for 4mm ribbon, the most readily available size.

As with fabric and embroidery floss, you will probably want to work with a limited color palette for ribbon. The colors you choose for the silk-ribbon flowers and leaves should coordinate closely with the rest of the quilt.

To create multi-shaded, realistic flowers and leaves, try variegated or hand-dyed silk ribbon dyed with different colors or different shades of the same color. The variations in color and shading add a dimension to silk-ribbon embroidery that solid colors cannot.

Here's a good rule of thumb: Choose three distinct shades of one color, ranging from dark to light, for the roses and other flowers, adding one or two accent colors for flower centers and buds. For the leaves, choose two shades of green silk ribbon that coordinate with your flosses and fabrics.

It's hard to estimate how much ribbon you need for this quilt; everyone stitches with a different amount of tension. Try making a sample piece of, say, a few berry clusters and a selection of different flowers, and keep track of how much ribbon you use as you stitch. Use this amount as a rough estimate for calculating the ribbon needed.

A size 18 Chenille needle works well for silk-ribbon embroidery. You should try different sizes, however, until you find the one comfortable for you. The larger the needle, the bigger the hole it will make in the fabric and the less wear and tear it will cause on the ribbon. Use 12" lengths of ribbon for stitching; this length reduces the tendency of the ribbon to fray and tear.

If your silk ribbon is wrinkled or creased, use a curling iron to press it. Just clip the ribbon in the curling iron and draw it through for a perfectly ironed ribbon.

Coloring Silk Ribbon

You can buy variegated or hand-dyed silk ribbon (see "Resources" on page 110), or you can make your own. I've included instructions for silk paint, which is safer and easier to use than silk dye. Always follow the manufacturer's instructions and safety precautions. I do not recommend dyeing or painting synthetic silk; it won't give you good results.

Using Silk Paint

Silk and fabric paints are made up of pigment in a gluelike base. This base bonds the pigment to the fiber, slightly stiffening the ribbon or fabric in the process. For lighter shades, thin the paint with water. Experiment with blending paints to create new colors.

1. Cut silk ribbon into 12"-long pieces.
2. Dampen the ribbon with water.
3. Using a small paintbrush, paint the ribbon.
4. Preheat your iron to a silk setting, then iron the ribbon until dry and the paint is set. Be sure to test for colorfastness (see directions at right).

Using Silk Dye

Unlike silk paint, silk dye does not affect the feel of the ribbon because the dye molecules form a chemical bond with the silk fibers. Any silk dye will work, as long as the ribbon is 100% silk.

Silk dye must be steam-set or dipped in a chemical fixative to be colorfast. Follow the manufacturer's instructions and safety precautions.

If you want to add a little gold or silver sparkle to your ribbon, use metallic air-brush paint formulated for fabrics. (These paints can be found in art-supply stores.) In a small spray-pump bottle, mix one part metallic air-brush paint with six parts water. Place the cap on the bottle and shake well. Immediately mist your 12" ribbon lengths with a light coating of the paint-and-water mixture. Don't overspray, or the ribbon will become too stiff to use for embroidery. Use an iron set to the "silk" setting to press the ribbon dry and set the paint. Now your ribbon is ready to use.

TESTING FOR COLORFASTNESS

Unless you are never going to wash your blocks or quilt, you should test the colorfastness of your thread and silk ribbon. It's better to be safe than sorry! (Refer to page 8 for instructions on testing fabric.) To test thread or silk ribbon, wet a small piece and pat it dry with a white paper towel. If you see any dye or color on the paper towel, the piece is not colorfast. Purples and deep reds are the worst culprits here.

You can rinse out excess dye by soaking the thread, silk ribbon, or braid in warm water, changing the water until it stays clear. Or try setting the dye, as described below.

1. Combine ¼ cup vinegar, ¾ cup warm water, and ¼ teaspoon salt in a glass measuring cup.
2. Gently swish the thread, silk ribbon, or braid around in the saltwater solution. If the water remains clear, you should be able to use the piece. If the dye bleeds, repeat the process until the water stays clear.
3. Air-dry and iron as necessary.

BEADS

Each of the Basket and Cornucopia motifs in this book is accented with small embroidery beads, size 11/0. Craft and fabric stores carry a wide array of beads for cross-stitch projects; these beads are the perfect size for your quilt. Choose beads that coordinate with your Basket and Cornucopia fabrics, then scatter these throughout the quilt.

Use strong quilting thread for beading, but choose a color that blends with the appliqué fabric, not the bead. You can also purchase special beading thread—a very strong, waxed nylon that reminds me of dental floss. It is available in white or black. Choose the color that best blends with your fabrics.

BATTING

Once you've assembled the quilt top, you will need batting. For best results, use a low-loft batting; the batting size depends on the size of your quilt top. I generally recommend cutting the batting 1" to 3" larger than the quilt top on all sides. Measure your quilt top to determine the size you need.

Tools

ROTARY-CUTTING EQUIPMENT

I recommend that you use a rotary cutter, cutting guide, and self-healing mat for cutting the background squares and border strips and trimming the blocks. These tools make cutting and trimming faster and easier. If you prefer, use fabric scissors.

EMBROIDERY SCISSORS

A pair of sharp embroidery scissors is essential; the appliqués in these blocks are tiny and detailed! A small, sharp pair of scissors will make it easier for you to cut out the appliqué pieces.

NEEDLES

You need several types of needles to make your miniature quilt. If you are new to embroidery, choose a package of needles that includes an assortment of sizes. Experiment with different sizes until you find a needle you feel comfortable using. As a general rule, the smaller the needle, the smaller the stitch you can make.

Appliqué (Sharp): Use appliqué needles, or Sharps, to tack or gather silk ribbon. (I also use these needles for beading.) Appliqué needles are thin enough to pass through beads, yet don't bend like beading needles.

Chenille: Cotton fabric's tight weave can stress silk ribbon; avoid this by using a large needle, such as a size 18 Chenille. Because a larger needle makes a bigger hole in the fabric, the ribbon is less likely to fray or shred as you stitch.

Embroidery: I like to use a size 8 Embroidery needle. It's small, but the eye is large enough for two strands of floss or decorative thread.

Quilting (Between): Commonly referred to as Betweens, these small needles are perfect for fine hand quilting. The smaller the needle, the smaller the stitches. If you are a beginning quilter, try a size 10.

Tapestry: These needles work well for woven-ribbon embroidery and can be used for silk-ribbon embroidery. While the blunt point won't snag the ribbon, it is much harder to push through the cotton fabric. A size 22 needle works well.

MARKING PENCILS

Use water-soluble markers, such as dressmakers' chalk, to transfer block designs to your background fabric. Be sure to use marking pencils that wash out—wax-based marking pencils may set when you iron the appliqués to your background fabric. If so, you won't be able to wash the marks out. For best results, test each marking pencil on scraps before using it with your projects.

Use a pencil or permanent-ink black marker to trace block designs onto paper-backed fusible web.

OPTIONAL TOOLS

Embroidery hoop: Try working with and without a hoop to see what works best for you. One advantage of working with a hoop is that it eliminates puckering in the background fabric. (If you choose to work without a hoop, you can remedy puckering by blocking your quilt blocks, as described on page 92.) One disadvantage of working with a hoop is that some silk-ribbon and embroidery stitches are more awkward to do.

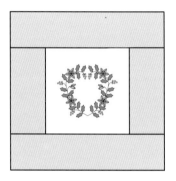

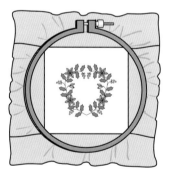

Thimble: I refuse to quilt without a thimble, but I don't use one while doing embroidery.

Awl: On a few blocks, you may need to stitch through all three layers: appliqué piece, fusible web, and background fabric. This can be challenging. Try using an awl to make a small hole in the fabric before stitching; this makes it easier to pull thread and ribbon through the fabric.

Fabric glue: If you have an appliqué piece that won't stay after fusing, anchor it in place with a bit of permanent-bond fabric glue.

CONSTRUCTING THE BLOCKS

By this time, you should know how many blocks will be in your quilt and you should have the fabrics cut for each block. If your blocks will include either of the two frame designs, it's easiest to appliqué the frames to the background square before marking the block pattern. This way, you can center the embroidery pattern in the frame rather than worrying about centering the frame around an already stitched design.

Working with Framed Blocks
MARKING THE FRAMES

To mark framed blocks, you need: one square of fabric for each frame you will use, cut to the same size; a marking pencil that is visible on your fabrics; pins or tape; and the frame patterns (see Appendix A, "Frame Patterns," on pages 104–5).

1. Fold each square into quarters, then finger-press the folds to make a grid.
2. Using the gridlines, center the outer frame fabric over the pattern. Pin or tape the fabric to the pattern so it will not shift as you work. It is very important that framed blocks be marked accurately and consistently.

Trace the appliqué lines onto the fabric, using your marking pencil. If you cannot see to mark the lines through the fabric, use a light box (see page 14), or make a plastic template of the pattern for tracing.

If you are making the double border, mark the middle frame next. You'll want to trace both the outer and inner appliqué lines on this fabric.

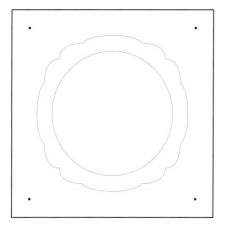

It isn't necessary to mark the frame pattern on your background fabric unless you want the added assurance of aligning everything. The appliqué should still be accurate without a marked background.

APPLIQUÉING THE FRAMES

For each block, you need: one background square and the marked frame square(s), scissors, basting thread that contrasts with the fabrics or small safety pins, sewing thread that matches the frame fabric, and an appliqué needle (Sharp).

1. Trim the excess fabric from the center of the frame, leaving a little less than a ¼" seam allowance all the way outside the marked line.

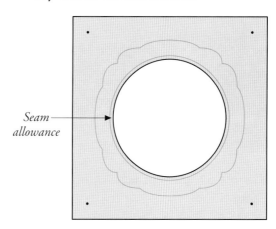

Seam allowance

2. Lay the frame fabric, right side up, on the background square, making sure the finger-pressed folds and the outside edges of each piece line up perfectly. (If you are making the double frame, you will be using the middle frame fabric here.) Baste the 2 squares together with contrasting thread, or pin-baste from behind with small brass safety pins.

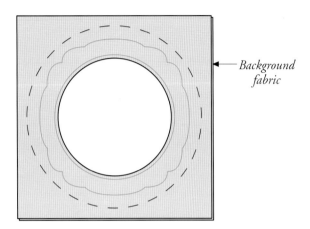

Background fabric

3. Appliqué the frame fabric to the background fabric, using matching thread and clipping curves. (Refer to Appendix C, "Needleturn Appliqué," on page 00 for appliqué instructions.) After you have appliquéd the block, turn it over and trim the excess fabric, leaving a ¼" seam allowance.
4. Continue this process for each of the blocks. (If you are making the double frame, repeat for the outer-frame fabric.)

After the framing is complete, you will be ready to trace the block patterns.

TRACING THE BLOCK PATTERNS

You need: one 6" square of background fabric for each block, pins or tape, and a water-soluble marking pencil. Test your marking pencil before you begin, to make sure it will wash out.

1. Fold a square of background fabric into quarters and finger-press the folds to make a grid.
2. Using the gridlines, center the fabric square on the placement guide. Pin or tape the fabric to the placement guide so it will not shift as you work.
3. Trace the placement guide.

If you cannot see the placement guide through your fabric, use a window or light table to help transfer the pattern. Tape the pattern and fabric to a sunny window. (I've even used the TV screen in a pinch!) If you don't have a light table, you can rig a makeshift one easily: just place a piece of glass between the leaves of a table and position a lamp underneath.

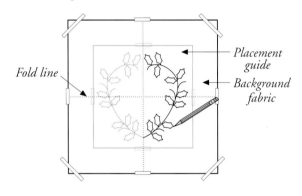

Fold line *Placement guide* *Background fabric*

Make your own light table.

TRACING THE APPLIQUÉS

This book describes the traditional method of tracing and fusing appliqués, as well as an alternative method I use in my classes.

Traditional Method

You need: the appliqué fabrics for your block, paper-backed fusible web, a pencil, an iron and ironing surface, small embroidery scissors, tweezers or pins, and the marked background-fabric square. You may find it easiest to trace and fuse the appliqués one block at a time, to avoid mixing up the pieces.

Always trace the appliqué patterns on the smooth paper side of the fusible web. (The fusible-web side feels slightly nubby.) Follow these steps for all the block patterns:

1. Using a pencil and the template sheets, trace all of the appliqué pieces onto the paper side of the fusible web. Group appliqués that are the same or that will be fused to the same fabric.

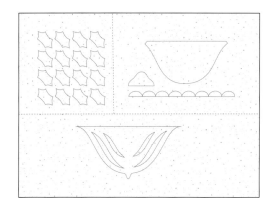

2. Cut the appliqué groups apart. Referring to the manufacturer's instructions, fuse one section to the wrong side of its appliqué fabric. Repeat for each section.

3. Using small embroidery scissors, cut out the appliqué pieces. If you are working with a piece that has small openings, such as the loops in a bow, remove these first before cutting out the rest of the piece.

4. Working as gently as possible, peel the paper backing from the appliqués. Take care not to fray the fabric, or the pieces may not fuse properly. I have found that if you let the appliqués sit for a half hour or so to cool completely, the paper will usually fall away. If you still have trouble, score the paper with a pin (this cuts the paper, not the fabric). Fold the appliqué in half along the scored line and grab a loose end of paper to peel off.

5. Following the placement guide marked on your background fabric, use tweezers to place the pieces accurately. Fuse in place, making sure the pieces are securely fastened to the background. Fabric glue should be used only as a last resort for stray appliqué pieces. Don't use glue for the entire quilt; it makes it too stiff.

Alternative Method

This sticker method, which I use in my classes, is a little simpler than traditional appliqué techniques. It also saves tracing time! You need full-page sticker label sheets. I suggest Avery 8165, available at office-supply and copy stores.

You need: appliqué fabrics for your blocks, printed sticker sheets (see step 1 below), paper-backed fusible web, an iron and ironing surface, small embroidery scissors, tweezers or pins, and your marked background squares.

1. Have a copy shop copy the templates you need from this book onto the label side of the sticker sheets. If you are repeating any of the blocks in the quilt, you will need duplicates of that sheet or design.

2. At home, cut apart the sticker sheet of your chosen block. Work with only 1 block at a time.

3. Group appliqués that will be fused to the same fabric, but do not trim them to size. Cut pieces of fusible web slightly larger than the stickers and fuse them to the wrong sides of the appropriate fabrics. Peel the sticker from the paper and place it on the paper side of the fusible web.

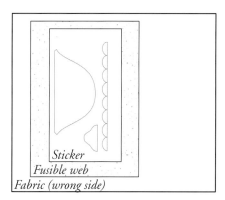

4. Follow steps 3–5 (at left) of "Traditional Method" to cut the appliqué pieces and fuse them to the background fabric.

EMBROIDERING YOUR BLOCKS

Once the appliqués have been fused to your blocks, it's time to embroider. Use the illustrations and photographs as guides when choosing flower size and placement. Before you start adding flowers, though, you may want to lay the block over the pattern and mark a few guidelines for flower placement. Since everyone stitches with a different tension, your flowers may not turn out exactly like the ones in the photos. If you have a basket with obvious open spaces, feel free to add a few smaller flowers, buds, or more leaves.

The stitch guide in this book includes all the embroidery stitches you need to outline the appliqués and make silk-ribbon flowers for the blocks, as well as general beading instructions. More flower instructions are included in individual block patterns. You'll also want to refer to "Embroidery Floss and Thread" on page 10 for suggestions. If you have not done any embroidery before, I recommend practicing on a sample piece of fabric first. Label the finished stitches on the fabric, and save this sample as a future guide.

Since you are probably working with a limited color palette, you might want to make some of your flowers from more than one shade of ribbon. Refer to the notes with each pattern and to the gallery on pages 17–40 for stitches that will look nicest in multiple shades.

Basic Instructions

1. Prepare a block, marking the embroidery pattern and fusing on the appliqués.
2. Embroider around all the leaves and stem lines. If the block includes a basket or other motif, embroider around those.
3. Press the block, face down on a terry cloth towel, to temporarily "block" the piece. This will help remove any puckers in your fabric before you add the silk-ribbon flowers and embellishments.
4. If you are working on a basket block, add the beading to the basket before you add the flowers. This will ensure a consistent line of beading, and the flowers will not be in the way.

5. Use silk ribbon to embroider all the berries and rosebuds, along with their leaves.
6. Stitch the silk-ribbon flowers for the block. If you are filling a basket, start with any background greenery, then stitch the central flower. This ensures that the major flower is placed correctly in the center, with the other flowers nicely framing it. It also makes choosing and adjusting the size of the flowers a little easier.
7. Stitch any remaining silk-ribbon leaves desired.

For more information on making blocks, refer to "Constructing the Blocks" on pages 13–15.

Embroidery Hints

❋ Outline all the appliqués with embroidery stitches, using two strands of floss.

❋ Use 12" to 18" lengths of floss or ribbon to avoid the frustration of tangles and fraying. I strongly recommend using 12" pieces, because silk ribbon frays easily.

❋ Keep an eye on the back of your block. There is nothing more frustrating than catching stitches on the back of the block and pulling out a previous stitch in the process. Train yourself to feel previous stitches and knots, and you'll avoid this problem.

❋ If the instructions for your block call for more than one type of one ribbon or floss, have both ready and threaded before you begin. It is much easier to have everything ready to use than to put the block down and thread a second needle.

❋ Neat and even embroidery stitches are more important than small stitches. Granted, you would like small stitches, but your blocks will look much nicer if you strive to make your stitches consistent.

❋ Weave the ends of your embroidery floss through the stitches on the back of the block. This will keep the tails from shadowing through the front.

GALLERY

A Silk Ribbon Album
by Jenifer Buechel, 1997,
Library, Pennsylvania, 32" x 32".

Christmas in Bloom
by Jenifer Buechel, 1998,
Library, Pennsylvania, 21½" x 21½";
quilted by Jill Dodin. The snowflake
background fabric complements the
theme of this quilt. To add sparkle, I
combined metallic thread with the
green embroidery floss.

Framed for Christmas
by Jenifer Buechel, 1998,
Library, Pennsylvania, 32" x 32";
quilted by Jill Dodin.

For My Best Friend
by Robin Giehll, 1998, Library, Pennsylvania,
24⅜" x 24⅜". Robin's quilt shines with Victorian flair.
The ornamental initial in the medallion
makes this a unique heirloom.

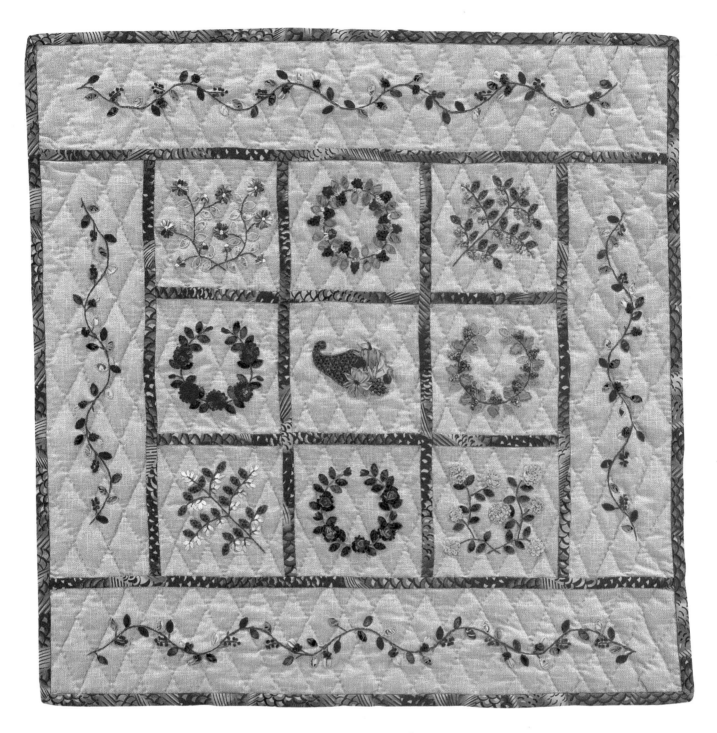

Autumn in My Garden
by Janet Wigg, 1998, Edinboro, Pennsylvania,
23" x 23". Inspired by her seasonal theme, Janet
substituted realistic autumn flowers for some
of the suggested stitches in the blocks.

Whig Roses and Wreaths
by Jenifer Buechel, 1998,
Library, Pennsylvania, 31" x 31";
quilted by Joy Mays.

Elegant Blossoms
by Jenifer Buechel, 1998,
Library, Pennsylvania, 21" x 21";
embroidered by Ardeth Laake
and quilted by Jill Dodin.

Memories of Mom
by Jenifer Buechel, 1998,
Library, Pennsylvania, 35" x 35";
quilted by Joy Mays.

Heart and Soul
by Mary Anne Lipinski, 1998,
Pittsburgh, Pennsylvania, 32" x 32".
Mary Anne's wonderful color selections
make this quilt stunning—
the outer-frame fabric was the
inspiration for the color palette.
Notice how the beading along the
frame edge accentuates the design.

Silver Baskets
by Mary Anne Lipinski, 1998,
Pittsburgh, Pennsylvania, 15½" x 15½".
Notice all the beaded embellishments and
how the sculptured binding fits the
mood of this elegant quilt.

Autumn Baskets
by Susan Gilbert, 1998,
Westbrook, Maine,
13½" x 13½". Rich autumn
colors glow in this small wall
hanging. Notice how the
sashing around the blocks
highlights Sue's
color choices.

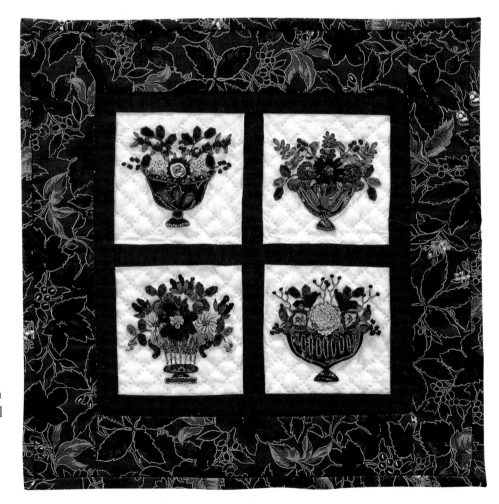

Friendship Basket
by Nancy Howard, Marcia de Rosas, Edith Kindred, Nancy Maher, Ellen O'Sullivan, Mary Shea, and Mary Anne Wedlock, 1998, Cambridge, Massachusetts, 25" x 25". Under the expert guidance of Nancy Howard, this beautiful wall hanging was completed in two months. Wonderfully coordinated throughout, it will proudly hang in Mary Anne's Shop, the Knittin' Kitten.

Black Beauty
by Nancy Howard, 1998, Cambridge, Massachusetts, 19" x 19". Nancy's expertly chosen ribbons and fabrics leap off the black background. Note that she used a partial border design to frame the corners of the quilt.

GALLERY OF BLOCKS

Medallion (page 55)

Block 1 (page 58)

Block 2 (page 59)

Block 3 (page 60)

Block 4 (page 61)

Block 5 (page 62)

Block 6 (page 63)

Block 7 (page 64)

Block 8 (page 65)

Block 9 (page 66)

Block 10 (page 67)

Block 11 (page 68)

Block 12 (page 70)

Block 13 (page 71)

Block 14 (page 72)

Block 15 (page 73)

Block 16 (page 74)

Block 17 (page 75)

Block 18 (page 76)

Block 19 (page 78)

Block 20 (page 79)

Block 21 (page 80)

Block 22 (page 81)

Block 23 (page 82)

Block 24 (page 83)

Block 25 (page 84)

Block 26 (page 85)

Block 27 (page 86)

Block 28 (page 87)

Block 29 (page 88)

Block 30 (page 89)

Block 31 (page 90)

Block 32 (page 91)

STITCHES AND FLOWERS

Threading and Knotting Silk Ribbon

To save ribbon, thread and knot as described below.

1. Thread one end of the ribbon through the eye of the needle.
2. Take the tip of the needle through one end of the ribbon.

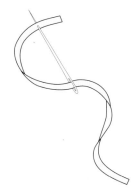

3. Pull the ribbon until it locks on the eye.
4. To put a knot in the other end of the ribbon, take a stitch in and out of the ribbon.

5. Slide the stitch down the length of the ribbon; a knot will form at the end.

BACKSTITCH

Use this stitch as a foundation for the whipped backstitch (page 53).

1. Bring the needle up at point A and down at point B.
2. Bring the needle up again at point C, then continue.

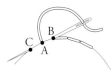

BULLION STITCH

Use this stitch to make a round bullion rose (page 42).

1. Bring the needle up at point A and down at point B. Bring the tip of the needle up again at point A, leaving it in the fabric, facing away from you.
2. Wrap embroidery floss or silk ribbon around the tip of the needle 5 to 8 times, depending on the length of the stitch between point A and point B. If you are using silk ribbon, keep the ribbon flat against the needle.
3. Gently pull the floss or ribbon through the wraps. (I like to use my thumb to hold the wraps on the needle as I pull the floss or ribbon through.) Take the needle down at point B.
4. Gently tug on the floss or ribbon to make sure the wraps are evenly distributed along the stitch.

 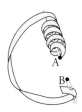

BULLION-TIPPED DAISY

Use this stitch to make leaves and flower petals with a pointed tip.

1. Bring the needle up at point A and down again just in front of point A. Bring the tip of the needle up at point B, leaving the needle in the fabric.
2. Wrap the embroidery floss or silk ribbon around the needle 3 times. If you are using silk ribbon, keep the ribbon flat against the needle.
3. Gently pull the floss or ribbon through the wraps. (Use your thumb to hold the wraps on the needle as you pull the floss or ribbon through.) Take the needle down at point C, just beyond the bullion tip at point B.

ROUND BULLION ROSE

Try substituting whipstitches (page 53) for the bullion stitches in this rose.

1. Make French knots (page 45), or stitch beads for the flower center.
2. Following the instructions for the bullion stitch (page 41), make bullion stitches for the petals, spiraling out around the flower center as you go.

BUTTONHOLE STITCH

This stitch is the basis for the pinwheel flower (page 48).

1. Bring the needle up at point A, down at point B, then up again at point C.
2. Repeat.

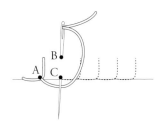

CHAIN STITCH

1. Bring the needle up at point A, down just behind point A, then up at point B.
2. For the next stitch, take the needle down just behind point B (inside the loop) and up at point C.
3. Repeat as desired. To finish, bring the needle to the back of the fabric, over the loop of the last chain.

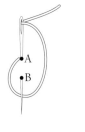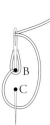

HEAVY CHAIN STITCH

This stitch is used to simulate the weave of baskets. You may want to increase the number of strands of floss to three or four, to make a more braidlike stitch.

1. Make a small straight stitch (page 52), up at point A and down at point B. Bring the needle up at point C.
2. Take the needle under the straight stitch, without catching the stitch or the fabric, and take the needle down again at point C.
3. Make additional chains by bringing the needle up at point D, taking the needle between the fabric and the previous chain, and going down again at point D.
4. Repeat step 3 until you reach the length you need.

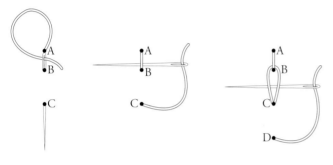

CHAIN STITCH ROSE

1. Stitch 3 French knots (page 45) to make the flower center.
2. Work chain stitches in a spiral around the French knots until the rose is the desired size. For a fuller flower, keep your chain stitches loose.

COLONIAL KNOT

This stitch is used for all the berries in the quilt. It makes a tiny ball, rounder than a French knot.

1. Bring the ribbon to the front and form a backward *C*.
2. Take the needle down into the backward *C* and wrap the ribbon over and under the needle, away from the eye, forming a figure-eight.
3. Pull the ribbon so it is snug on the needle. Push the loaded needle down to the back of the block, as close as possible to the point it originally came up.

CORAL STITCH ROSE

For this stitch, keep the tension loose.

1. Stitch 3 French knots (page 45) to make the flower center.
2. Bring the needle up at point A, down at point B, and up again at point C, wrapping the embroidery floss or silk ribbon over and under the needle.
3. Gently pull the floss or ribbon until a loose knot forms. (These loose knots form the petals of the rose.)
4. Continue stitching in a spiral, bringing the needle down at point D and up at point E, wrapping the floss or ribbon over and under the needle each time.

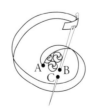 

COUCHED LOOP ROSE

Couch this looped flower with matching thread.

1. Stitch 3 to 5 French knots (page 45) to make the flower center.
2. Thread a 12"-long piece of silk ribbon on one needle and a matching colored thread on a second needle.
3. Bring both needles up at point A at the same time.
4. Form a loop of ribbon for the first petal.
5. With the matching thread, couch the ribbon petal, catching the ribbon edge at point B.
6. Bring the needle with the matching thread up again close to point A. Form another loop of ribbon and couch, catching the edge of the ribbon at point B.
7. Repeat until you've couched enough loops for your flower. Finish by knotting both the ribbon and thread on the back of the block.

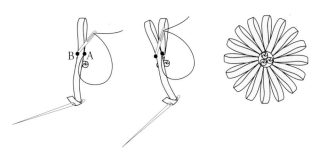

CROSS-STITCH FLOWER

Use this tiny flower as filler whenever you need a few small flowers.

1. Bring the needle up at point A, down at point B, then up at point C.
2. To finish the cross-stitch, take the needle down at point D.
3. To make the center of the flower, couch the center with a second color of embroidery floss or silk ribbon, bringing the needle up at point E and down at point F.

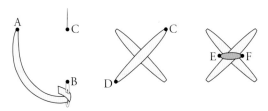

FEATHER STITCH

1. Bring the needle up at point A, down at point B, then up at point C.
2. Take the needle down at point D and up at point E. Continue as shown.

FISHBONE STITCH

This stitch is the basis for the fishbone flower.

1. Bring the needle up at point A, down at point B, then up at point C.
2. Take the needle down at point D.
3. Repeat. Keep the distance between points B and C, as well as the distance between points A and D, the same for each stitch.

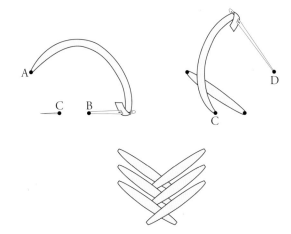

FLY STITCH

1. Bring the needle up at point A, down at point B, then up at point C.
2. Take the needle down at point D.

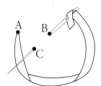

FRENCH KNOT

Use this versatile stitch for flower centers or groups of tiny buds. If you are using silk ribbon, the smaller the knot you want, the flatter you should wrap it around the needle. If you want a puffy knot, keep the tension loose and allow the ribbon to twist as you wrap it around the needle.

1. Bring the needle up at point A.
2. Wrap the floss, thread, or ribbon around the tip of the needle 3 times.
3. Take the needle down next to point A. Gently pull the floss or ribbon until a knot forms.

GATHERED RIBBON

1. Thread one needle with a 12"-long piece of silk ribbon; thread a second needle with matching thread.
2. Bring both needles up at point A.
3. Using the second needle, make a running stitch (page 50) along one edge of the ribbon as shown.
4. Gently gather the ribbon to the desired length. To tack in place, bring the second needle to the back of the block and knot the thread.
5. To finish, bring the first needle to the back and knot the ribbon.

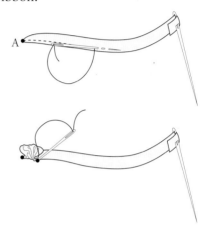

GATHERED ROSE

When using the traditional method, you first gather the length of ribbon, then tack the rose in place. I found this awkward when I was working with 4mm silk ribbon, so I adapted the traditional stitch to gather and tack at the same time.

1. Thread one needle with a 12"-long piece of silk ribbon and a second needle with matching thread.
2. Bring both needles up at point A. This spot will be the center of the rose.
3. Using the second needle and a running stitch (page 50), stitch approximately 1" along one selvage edge of the ribbon.
4. Gently gather the ribbon. To tack in place, bring the second needle down at point B and up at point C.
5. Repeat steps 3 and 4, working in a spiral around point A, until the rose is the desired size.
6. Bring both needles to the back and knot the ribbon and thread to finish.

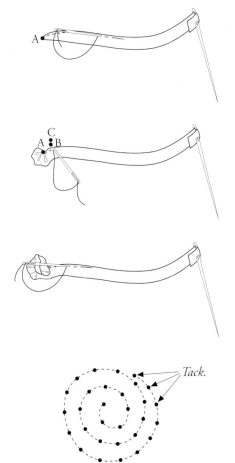

LAZY DAISY

Keep your loops as flat as possible.

1. Bring the needle up at point A, down at point B, then up again at point C. Make sure the embroidery floss or silk ribbon is under the needle, as shown.
2. Gently pull the floss or ribbon. Take the needle down at point D (tack stitch).

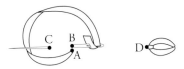

ELONGATED LAZY DAISY

Make a lazy daisy stitch (page 46), but elongate the tack stitch (point B to point C). If you are using silk ribbon, keep the tack stitch as flat as possible.

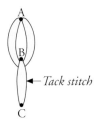

KNOTTED LAZY DAISY

1. Bring the needle up at point A, down at point B, then up at point C.
2. Wrap the ribbon around the needle as you would for a French knot (page 45).
3. Bring the ribbon down at point D, forming a knot on the lazy daisy.

PIGGYBACKED LAZY DAISY

1. Thread a needle with ribbon; thread a second needle with coordinating ribbon. Bring one needle up at point A.
2. Take the same needle down at point A, forming a loop. Do not pull the ribbon all the way through, and try to keep it flat.
3. Bring the second ribbon up at point B (inside the first loop), down at point B, then up at point C, making a lazy daisy stitch at the tip of the first loop. (This stitch should be smaller than the first loop.)
4. Tack the second ribbon at point D. Gently pull the first stitch until it is snug but not tight, and secure both ribbons on the back of the block.

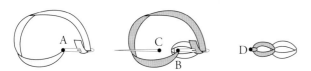

TACKED LAZY DAISY

1. Thread a needle with ribbon; thread a second needle with coordinating floss.
2. Bring the needle with ribbon up at point A, then down at point A, leaving a loop on the front of the fabric. Try to keep the ribbon as flat as possible.
3. With the floss, make a tack stitch from point B to point C, over the loop.
4. Gently pull the ribbon loop until it is snug but not tight, and secure both the ribbon and floss on the back of the block.

LOOP STITCH

This is just one method for making a loop stitch. It works well for leaves and flower petals.

1. Bring the needle up at point A.
2. To create a loop, lay the ribbon on itself as shown. Take the needle down through both layers of ribbon at point B.
3. Gently pull the ribbon through the layers until snug. If you pull the ribbon too tight, the loop will pull through the fabric. (I like to hold the loop on the front with my thumb as I pull the ribbon through.)

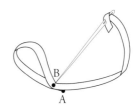

KNOTTED OPEN LOOP STITCH

This loop stitch variation has a knot at the tip of each loop, giving the open loop stitch (see right) a little twist.

1. Bring the ribbon up at point A and form a loop, keeping the ribbon flat.
2. Pierce the ribbon at the halfway point of the loop with the needle, and pull the ribbon partway through. Take the needle back through the newly formed loop and pull until the knot is snug but not tight.
3. Take the needle down at point B, keeping the 2 sides of the loop flat and side by side. There is nothing anchoring the loop at this point, so be careful not to pull it out.
4. Bring the needle up at point C, through the last loop, to begin the next stitch and secure the first loop.

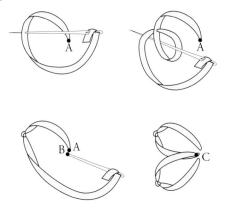

OPEN LOOP STITCH

1. Bring the needle up at point A and form a loop, keeping the ribbon flat.
2. Take the needle down at point B. Keep the same side of ribbon facing you at all times and make sure the 2 sides of the loop are next to each other. There is nothing anchoring the loop at this point, so be careful not to pull it out.
3. To secure the previous stitch and make the next loop, bring the needle up at point C, through the last leg of the stitch. Continue to make loops.

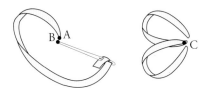

PINWHEEL FLOWER

If you want multiple rows of petals in this flower, work the rows from the outside in. That way, the inner rows are laid on top of previous rows, and you're not trying to stitch from underneath.

1. Work a buttonhole stitch (page 42) in a circle for the outer row of petals.
2. Stitch smaller succeeding rows on top of the first row.

PISTIL STITCH

1. Bring the needle up at point A.
2. About ½" down the ribbon, wrap as you would to make a French knot (page 45).
3. Take the needle to the back at point B, and pull the ribbon snug to form a knot.

PLUME STITCH

1. Bring the needle up at point A and form a loop.
2. At the base of the loop, catching only the front of the loop and a bit of the background fabric, take a very small tack stitch from point B to point C. Pull the ribbon through.
3. Continue making loops and tacking them down, working the stitch toward yourself.
4. To finish, make a tack stitch, taking the ribbon to the back, and knot the ribbon.

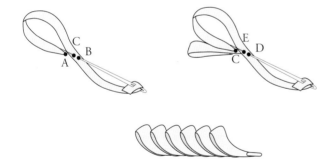

RIBBON STITCH

This is one of the easiest silk-ribbon stitches. Use it to make leaves or flowers.

1. Bring the needle up at point A.
2. Lay the ribbon flat, then take the needle down through the ribbon at point B.
3. Gently pull the ribbon through until the sides curl up to form a leaf shape.

ROSETTE CHAIN FLOWER

Keep your tension loose as you stitch.

1. Bring the needle up at point A, down at point B, then up at point C.
2. Push the needle under the stitch next to point A.
3. Repeat the stitch, working to the left and taking the needle down at point D, then up again at point E.

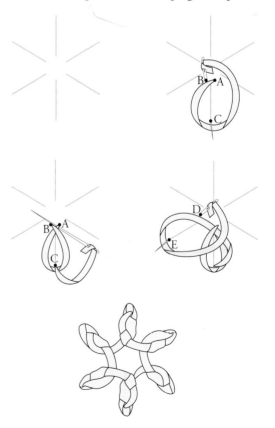

RUCHED ROSE

These roses are lovely and always seem to attract a great deal of attention. However, it takes patience and persistence to make them. Don't be surprised if it takes twenty minutes just to gather the ribbon.

1. Cut a 12"-long piece of ribbon. Thread an appliqué needle with matching thread.

2. Using a running stitch (page 50), stitch back and forth across the width of the ribbon as shown. Make sure the thread goes over the edge of the ribbon at each turn.

3. As you stitch, gently pull the thread to gather the ribbon. Don't let the gathers twist. Check to make sure you have a set of petals on either side of the gathers.

4. To tack the rose to the fabric, stitch one end of the ribbon in place for the flower center.

5. Spiral the gathered ribbon around the flower center, tacking the inner petals and leaving the outer petals free.

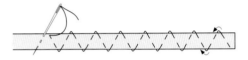

RUNNING (QUILTING) STITCH

1. Begin with a straight stitch (page 52). Bring the needle up at point A, the same distance away as the length of the straight stitch you just made.

2. Take the needle down at point B and up at point C. Make sure the stitches are even.

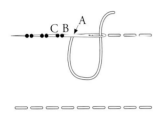

SCROLL STITCH ROSE

Keep your tension loose as you stitch.

1. Stitch 3 French knots (page 45) to make the flower center.

2. Bring the needle up at point A, down at point B, then up at point C.

3. Wrap the silk ribbon under the eye of the needle and under the tip as shown, then gently pull through.

4. Continue stitching in a spiral around the flower center. Repeat until rose is the desired size.

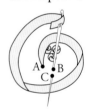

SPIDERWEB ROSE

This popular silk-ribbon rose is woven on a foundation stitch of five spokes. It's simple to complete.

1. Thread one needle with a 12"-long piece of silk ribbon and a second needle with matching thread.
2. Bring the second needle up at point A, down at point B, then up at point C, keeping the stitches even.
3. Bring the second needle down at point D.
4. Repeat steps 2 and 3, bringing the second needle up at the center and over to one side. Repeat, bringing the needle over to the other side for the last spoke. Knot the thread on the back of the block.
5. Bring the needle with the silk ribbon up near the center of the web. Weave the ribbon over and under the spokes without catching the spokes or the fabric. When the spokes are completely covered, knot the ribbon on the back of the block. If you have a slightly longer spoke that you can't cover with the ribbon, hide the end by adding a leaf. No one will ever know you made a mistake!

STEM STITCH

This stitch works well for outlining appliqués. Keep your thread on the side of the appliqué so the stitch will lie snugly against the edge of the fabric.

1. Make a small straight stitch (page 52). Bring the needle up at point A and down at point B, then up again halfway between points A and B, at point C.
2. Take the needle down at point D and up again at the end of the last stitch, point B.
3. Repeat, bringing the needle up at the end of each previous stitch.

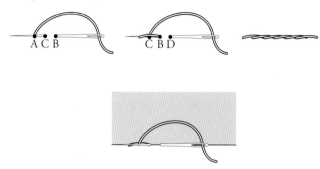

STEM STITCH ROSE

I've included two methods; the second makes a plumper rose.

Method 1

1. Make 3 French knots (page 45) or stitch beads for the flower center.
2. Work a stem stitch (above) around the French knots, spiraling outward until rose is the desired size.

Method 2

1. Work a stem stitch around the outside of the flower, spiraling inward to the center.
2. Stitch 3 French knots (page 45) to make the flower center.

STRAIGHT STITCH

If you are using silk ribbon, keep the ribbon as flat as possible. Bring the needle up at A and down at B.

TWISTED CHAIN STITCH

This stitch is perfect for silk-ribbon rosebuds.

1. Bring the needle up at point A and down at point B. Bring the tip of the needle up at point C, but do not pull the needle through.
2. Wrap the ribbon over and under the tip of the needle, as shown.
3. Pull the ribbon through at point C and down at point D.

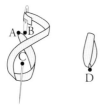

TWISTED CHAIN ROSE

Start at the center of the flower and work the twisted chain stitch (above) in a spiral. As you work the stitches, keep angling them outward.

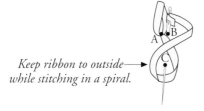

Keep ribbon to outside while stitching in a spiral.

TWISTED RIBBON ROSE

This rose will be different every time you make it. If your rose doesn't turn out the way you want, take out the stitch and iron the ribbon. For a larger bloom, add a row of stem stitches (page 51) around the rose.

1. Thread one needle with a 12"-long piece of silk ribbon and a second needle with matching thread.
2. Bring the needle with the ribbon up through the center of the rose (point A). Twist the ribbon until tight, but stop before it begins to kink.
3. Pinch the ribbon halfway down the twisted length and fold it in half.
4. Allow the two halves to twist together. Take the needle down at point B.
5. Gently pull the needle through the fabric, letting the twists form the rose.
6. Using the needle with matching thread, tack the rose to the block.

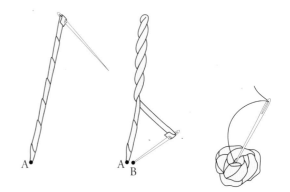

TWISTED RIBBON FLOWER

I discovered this flower while learning to make a twisted ribbon rose. I like the cone-shaped bloom.

1. Follow steps 1–4 for a twisted ribbon rose (page 52).
2. Gently pull the needle and ribbon through the fabric until a twisted cone forms.
3. Push the twisted cone on its side, against the fabric, and tack with matching thread.
4. Frame the flower with ribbon-stitch leaves (page 49).

WHIPPED BACKSTITCH

1. Thread two coordinating colors of ribbon on two different needles.
2. Work a loose backstitch (page 41) with one ribbon. Knot this ribbon on the back.
3. Bring the second ribbon up underneath the first backstitch. Take the ribbon under the next stitch without catching the backstitch or the fabric.
4. Continue to loosely whip over the backstitches, keeping the ribbon as flat as possible. Finish by knotting the second ribbon on the back of the block.

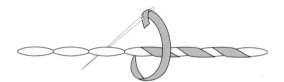

WHIPSTITCH

Vary the size of this bud by changing the length of the straight stitch or the number of wraps.

1. With one threaded needle, make straight stitches (page 52) the length of the desired bud.
2. Push the straight stitch aside and bring the needle up underneath the stitch.
3. Wrap embroidery floss, thread, or silk ribbon around the straight stitch. (You can use the same or a different needle.) If you are using silk ribbon, keep the ribbon as flat as possible.
4. To finish, push the stitch aside and bring the needle to the back of the block.

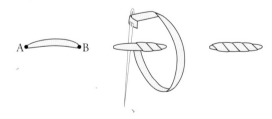

ADDING BEADS

There are many ways to attach beads to quilt blocks. This is my favorite method.

1. Bring the needle up through the fabric, through the bead, then down through the fabric. Repeat, stitching through the bead twice.

2. Slide the next bead onto the needle and repeat step 1.

3. Run the needle and thread back through the length of the beads to straighten them. Knot the thread on the back of the block.

BEADING THREAD

When choosing thread, pick a color that matches the background fabric rather than the beads. This way, the thread will blend with your background.

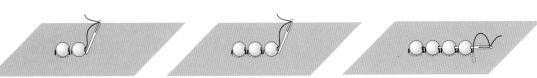

PATTERNS

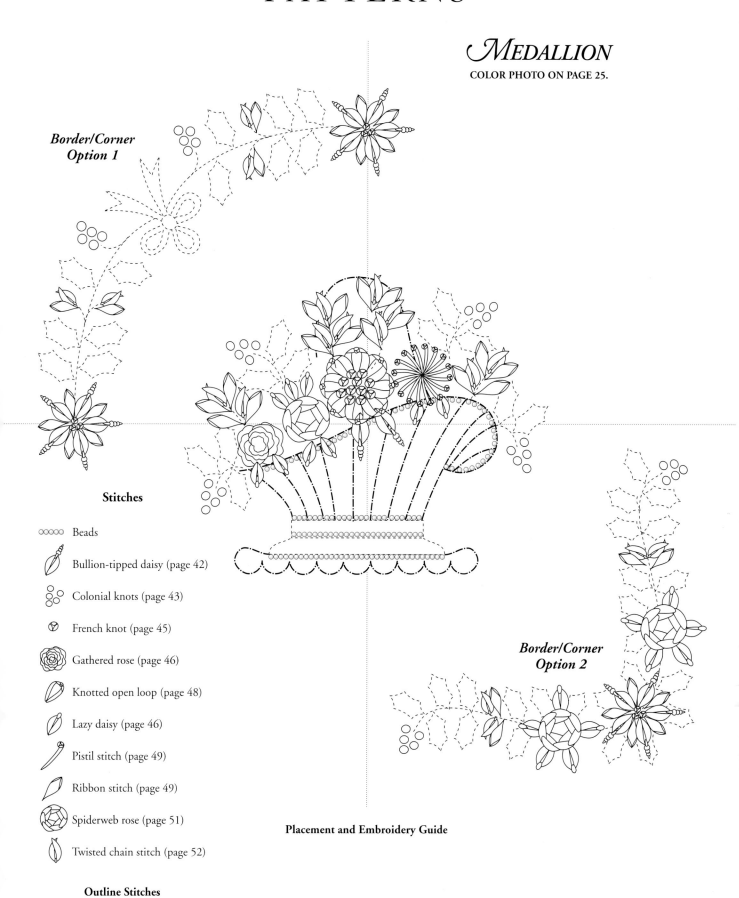

Medallion
COLOR PHOTO ON PAGE 25.

Border/Corner Option 1

Border/Corner Option 2

Placement and Embroidery Guide

Stitches

ᵒᵒᵒᵒᵒ Beads

Bullion-tipped daisy (page 42)

Colonial knots (page 43)

French knot (page 45)

Gathered rose (page 46)

Knotted open loop (page 48)

Lazy daisy (page 46)

Pistil stitch (page 49)

Ribbon stitch (page 49)

Spiderweb rose (page 51)

Twisted chain stitch (page 52)

Outline Stitches

—·—·— Heavy chain stitch (page 43)

- - - - - Stem stitch (page 51)

**Appliqué Pieces
for Medallion on Page 55**

POINSETTIA

Use more than one shade of ribbon for this flower to give it contrast.

1. Make 5 ribbon stitches, leaving room in the center for 3 French knots.
2. Add 5 bullion-tipped daisies, stitching them between each ribbon stitch.
3. Stitch 3 French knots in the center.

CENTRAL BASKET FLOWER

1. Make about 8 knotted open loop stitches in a circle, using 1 color of ribbon. Leave a space for French knots in the center.
2. Place a row of French knots, stitched from a second color of ribbon, directly on top of each leg of the loops. Stitch right on top of the ribbon.
3. Make a cluster of French knots to fill the center of the flower, using a third ribbon color.

BLOCK 1

COLOR PHOTO ON PAGE 25.

Work the stem stitch rose in two shades of ribbon. If you wish, add French knots at the center of the rose.

Stitches

   Colonial knots (page 43)

Ribbon stitch (page 49)

Stem stitch rose (page 51)

 Twisted chain stitch (page 52)

Outline Stitch

- - - - - Stem stitch (page 51)

Placement and Embroidery Guide

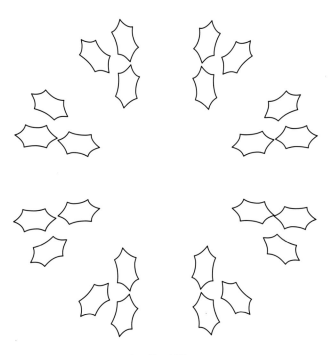

Appliqué Pieces

BLOCK 2

COLOR PHOTO ON PAGE 26.

To make a two-toned spiderweb rose, start weaving the rose with one color of ribbon. When the rose is approximately half-completed, knot that ribbon on the back and thread a needle with a different color. Finish weaving the rose, using the second color of ribbon.

Stitches

 Colonial knots (page 43)

 Spiderweb rose (page 51)

Outline Stitch

- - - - - Stem stitch (page 51)

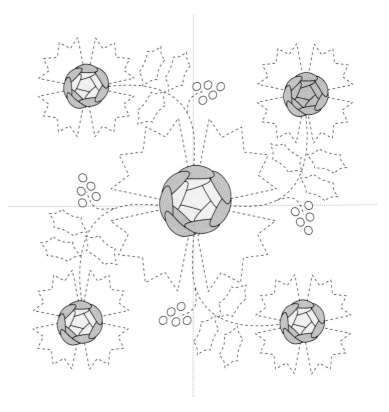

Placement and Embroidery Guide

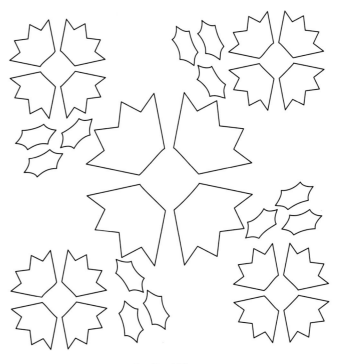

Appliqué Pieces

BLOCK 3

COLOR PHOTO ON PAGE 26.

Stitches

 Beads

Colonial knots (page 43)

Couched loop rose (page 44)

French knot (page 45)

Heavy chain stitch (ribbon) (page 43)

Lazy daisy (page 46)

Ribbon stitch (page 49)

Spiderweb rose (page 51)

Whipstitch (page 53)

Outline Stitches

—·—·— Heavy chain stitch (page 43)

- - - - - Stem stitch (page 51)

Placement and Embroidery Guide

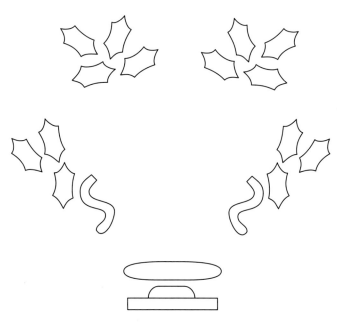

Appliqué Pieces

BLOCK 4

COLOR PHOTO ON PAGE 27.

Stitches

 Colonial knots (page 43)

French knot (page 45)

Ribbon stitch (page 49)

Round bullion rose (page 42)

Twisted chain stitch (page 52)

Outline Stitch

------ Stem stitch (page 51)

Placement and Embroidery Guide

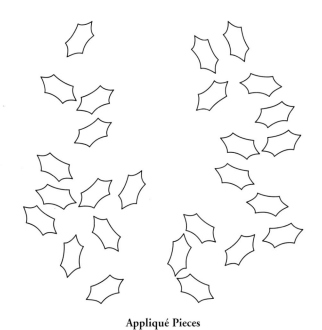

Appliqué Pieces

BLOCK 5

COLOR PHOTO ON PAGE 27.

If making ribbon-stitch flowers, you may want to mark 8 small guidelines on your fabric before stitching. Begin by making a French knot for the center of the flower. Following the instructions for the ribbon stitch, make eight petals around the flower center as shown. Be careful not to catch the ribbon on the back of the block; you could pull out the previous stitch.

Placement and Embroidery Guide

Stitches

 Colonial knots (page 43)

French knot (page 45)

Ribbon stitch (page 49)

Twisted chain stitch (page 52)

Outline Stitch

- - - - - - Stem stitch (page 43)

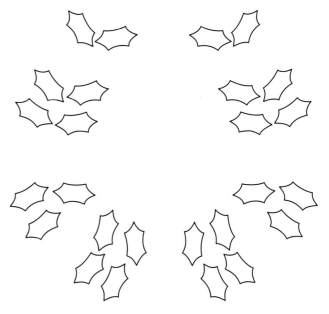

Appliqué Pieces

Block 6

COLOR PHOTO ON PAGE 28.

To make a multi-toned ruched rose, gather 2 or 3 lengths of ribbon, each ribbon a different color. Start with the lightest ribbon and tack it to the center, following the instructions for the rose on page 59. Add the additional colors as though you were using 1 long piece, tucking the raw ends under the rose.

You can also use two shades of ribbon for the pinwheel flower. Stitch the outer portion of the flower in one shade, then finish the inner petals with a second shade.

To show a secondary color through the cutwork design on the urn, fuse a fabric patch a little larger than the cutwork area to the corresponding spot on your marked background fabric. (Before fusing, make sure the patch is small enough to fit behind the urn pattern piece without showing.) Trim stray threads, then fuse the urn on top.

Placement and Embroidery Guide

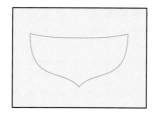

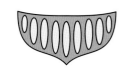

Stitches

 Beads

 Bullion-tipped daisy (page 42)

 Colonial knots (page 43)

Feather stitch—floss (page 44)

 French knot (page 45)

Pinwheel flower (page 48)

Ribbon stitch (page 49)

Ruched rose (page 50)

Twisted ribbon rose (page 52)

Outline Stitches

—·—·— Heavy chain stitch (page 43)

- - - - - Stem stitch (page 51)

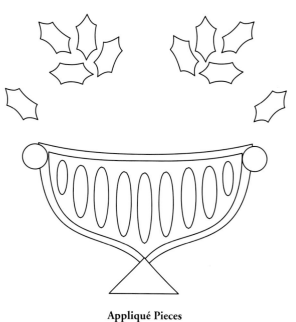

Appliqué Pieces

BLOCK 7

COLOR PHOTO ON PAGE 28.

Add interest to your gathered rose by using more than one color. Start with a light shade for the middle of the rose. Change to slightly darker ribbon shades as you work outward.

Stitches

Colonial knots (page 43)

Gathered rose (page 46)

Lazy daisy (page 46)

Outline Stitch

- - - - - Stem stitch (page 51)

Placement and Embroidery Guide

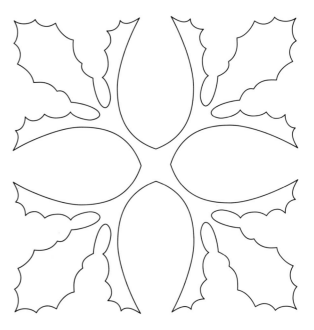

Appliqué Piece

Block 8

COLOR PHOTO ON PAGE 29.

Stitch

Colonial knots (page 43)

Outline Stitch

----- Stem stitch (page 51)

Placement and Embroidery Guide

Appliqué Pieces

Block 9

COLOR PHOTO ON PAGE 29.

Add a cutwork section to the urn, following the directions given for Block 6 (page 63).

To make the middle rose, work 8 piggybacked lazy daisies in two shades of ribbon, leaving a gap in the center of the grouped stitches. Add a gathered rose to the center of the flower, using a darker ribbon.

Placement and Embroidery Guide

Stitches

ooooo Beads

 Bullion-tipped daisy (page 42)

Colonial knots (page 43)

French knot (page 45)

Gathered rose (page 46)

Piggybacked lazy daisy (page 47)

Ribbon stitch (page 49)

 Twisted chain rose (page 52)

Whipstitch (page 53)

Outline Stitches

—·—·— Heavy chain stitch (page 43)

------ Stem stitch (page 51)

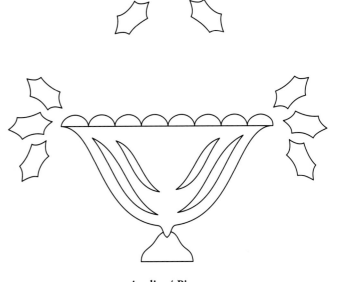

Appliqué Pieces

BLOCK 10

COLOR PHOTO ON PAGE 30.

Stitches

 Chain stitch rose (page 43)

 Colonial knots (page 43)

 French knot (page 45)

 Ribbon stitch (page 49)

 Twisted chain stitch (page 52)

Outline Stitch

- - - - - Stem stitch (page 51)

Placement and Embroidery Guide

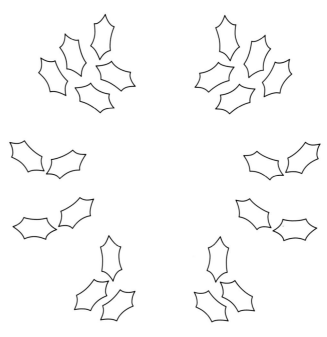

Appliqué Pieces

BLOCK 11

To make the middle flower, mark a ½"-diameter circle. You'll use this as a guide for the flower center. Embroider 16 ribbon-stitch petals evenly around the circle. Using a different shade of ribbon, work a series of 16 pistil stitches from the center of the flower, with the knot of each stitch on top of a ribbon petal base.

To make the lazy daisy flowers, start with a French knot for the center, then space 6 to 8 lazy daisy stitches evenly around the center. You may want to lightly mark guides on the fabric before stitching.

To make the ferns, mark a guideline for the stem. At the top of the line, make a small straight stitch, then make a fly stitch under the straight stitch. Continue adding fly stitches, gradually increasing the size of each. Make sure the center stitches touch so the stem appears to be continuous.

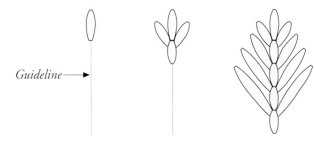

Guideline ⟶

Stitches

ooooo   Beads

Colonial knots (page 43)

Cross-stitch flower (page 44)

Fly stitch (page 45)

French knot (page 45)

Lazy daisy (page 46)

Pistil stitch (page 49)

Ribbon stitch (page 49)

Straight stitch (page 52)

Outline Stitches

—·—·—   Heavy chain stitch (page 43)

- - - - -   Stem stitch (page 51)

Placement and Embroidery Guide

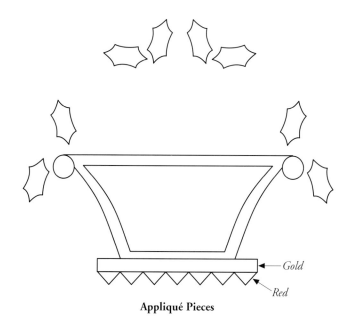

Gold

Red

Appliqué Pieces

BLOCK 12

COLOR PHOTO ON PAGE 31.

To make a loop-stitch flower, start with 3 French knots for the center. Work 8 loop stitches, spacing them evenly around the French knots. To make the loop stitches more durable and decorative, take a tack stitch at the base of each petal with contrasting embroidery floss.

Tackstitch in contrasting floss

Stitches

⊙⊙ Colonial knots (page 43)

⊘ French knot (page 45)

◁ Loop stitch (page 47)

◿ Ribbon stitch (page 49)

◊ Twisted chain stitch (page 52)

Outline Stitches

- - - - - Stem stitch (page 43)

——— Straight stitch (page 51)

Placement and Embroidery Guide

Appliqué Pieces

BLOCK 13

COLOR PHOTO ON PAGE 31.

The twisted ribbon combination for the flowers should be worked in two shades of ribbon. Make a twisted ribbon rose first, for the center of each flower. Bring your second shade of ribbon to the front, right beside the rose, and gather and tack, placing the gathers snugly beside the ribbon rose.

Stitches

 Colonial knots (page 43)

 Gathered ribbon (page 45)

 Ribbon stitch (page 49)

 Twisted chain stitch (page 52)

 Twisted ribbon rose (page 52)

Outline Stitch

- - - - - - Stem stitch (page 51)

Placement and Embroidery Guide

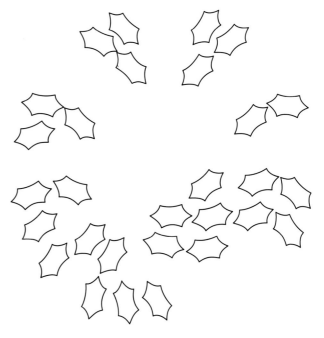

Appliqué Pieces

BLOCK 14

COLOR PHOTO ON PAGE 32.

Stitches

 Colonial knots (page 43)

French knot (page 45)

Ribbon stitch (page 49)

Scroll stitch rose (page 50)

Twisted chain stitch (page 52)

Outline Stitch

------ Stem stitch (page 51)

Placement and Embroidery Guide

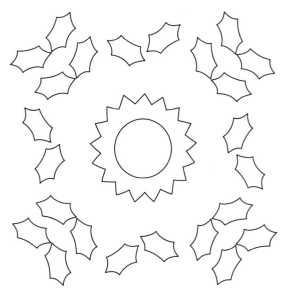

Appliqué Pieces

BLOCK 15

COLOR PHOTO ON PAGE 32.

For the middle loop-stitch variation, make eight loop stitches in a circle, leaving a small gap in the center of the flower. With a second color of ribbon, carefully make 1 ribbon stitch from the center of the flower directly on top of each loop-stitch petal. Make sure to stitch carefully so you don't pull out either the loop stitches or any previous ribbon stitches. Finish with a French knot in the middle of the flower.

Placement and Embroidery Guide

Stitches

 Colonial knots (page 43)

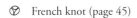 French knot (page 45)

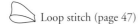 Loop stitch (page 47)

  Ribbon stitch (page 49)

  Twisted chain stitch (page 52)

Outline Stitch

- - - - - - Stem stitch (page 51)

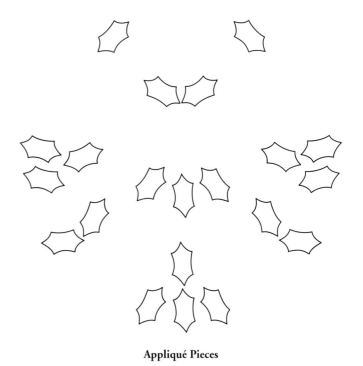

Appliqué Pieces

BLOCK 16

COLOR PHOTO ON PAGE 33

You may want to mark 6 guidelines for each flower to help space the petals evenly.

Stitches

 Colonial knots (page 43)

French knot (page 45)

Ribbon stitch (page 49)

Tacked lazy daisy (page 47)

Twisted chain stitch (page 52)

Outline Stitch

------ Stem stitch (page 51)

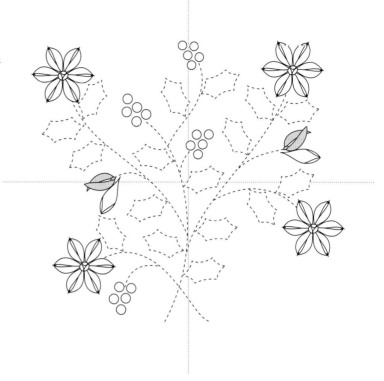

Placement and Embroidery Guide

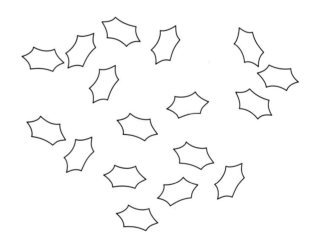

Appliqué Pieces

BLOCK 17

COLOR PHOTO ON PAGE 33.

Use two shades of ribbon for the ruched rose.

Stitches

 Colonial knots (page 43)

Ruched rose (page 50)

Outline Stitch

----- Stem stitch (page 51)

Placement and Embroidery Guide

Appliqué Pieces

BLOCK 18

COLOR PHOTO ON PAGE 34.

Add a cutwork section to the urn, following the directions given for Block 6 (page 63).

For a pretty spiderweb rose variation, begin with 5 elongated lazy daisies stitched from one shade of ribbon. The tack stitches should all meet in the center of the rose. Use the tack stitches as a foundation for weaving a spiderweb rose, using a second shade of ribbon. After the web is filled, add a few regular lazy daisy stitches between the elongated ones to complete the stitched circle around the rose.

The fuchsias are a variation of the knotted lazy daisy stitch. To make them, add a semicircle of gathered ribbon in a contrasting color, opposite the knot.

Stitches

 Beads

 Bullion-tipped daisy (page 42)

Colonial knots (page 43)

Coral stitch rose (page 43)

French knot (page 45)

Gathered ribbon (page 45)

Knotted lazy daisy (page 46)

Lazy daisy (page 46)

Ribbon stitch (page 49)

Spiderweb rose (page 51)

Stem stitch (ribbon) (page 51)

Outline Stitches
—·—·— Heavy chain stitch (page 43)
- - - - - Stem stitch (page 51)

Placement and Embroidery Guide

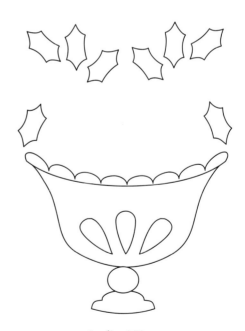

Appliqué Pieces

BLOCK 19

COLOR PHOTO ON PAGE 34.

Stitches

 Colonial knots (page 43)

 Couched loop rose (page 44)

French knot (page 45)

Ribbon stitch (page 49)

Twisted chain stitch (page 52)

Outline Stitch

- - - - - Stem stitch (page 51)

Placement and Embroidery Guide

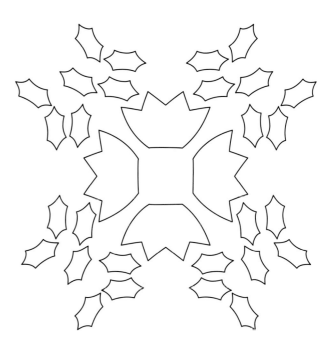

Appliqué Pieces

BLOCK 20

COLOR PHOTO ON PAGE 35.

To make the middle flower, draw a ½"-diameter circle for the center. Make 16 knotted loop stitches from one shade of ribbon, with the base of each leg sitting on the circle. Add a gathered ribbon rose to the center of the flower, using a lighter ribbon. Using darker ribbon, top each leg of the knotted loop stitches with a French knot, surrounding the gathered rose.

Placement and Embroidery Guide

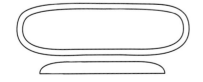

Appliqué Pieces

Stitches

 Beads

 Bullion-tipped daisy (page 42)

 Colonial knots (page 43)

 French knot (page 45)

 Gathered rose (page 46)

 Knotted open loop (page 48)

Lazy daisy (page 46)

 Plume stitch (page 49)

 Ribbon stitch (page 49)

 Stem stitch rose (page 51)

 Twisted chain stitch (page 52)

Outline Stitches

–·–·– Heavy chain stitch (page 43)

------ Stem stitch (page 51)

——— Straight stitch (page 52)

BLOCK 21

COLOR PHOTO ON PAGE 35.

For the center flower's open-loop combination, make 12 open-loop petals with one shade of ribbon. Leave a gap in the center of the flower. Using a second color, embroider a twisted ribbon flower in the gap, taking care not to pull out any of the previous stitches.

Placement and Embroidery Guide

Stitches

 Beads

 Bullion-tipped daisy (page 42)

 Colonial knots (page 43)

 Feather stitch (ribbon) (page 44)

 French knot (page 45)

 Lazy daisy (page 46)

 Open loop stitch (page 48)

 Ribbon stitch (page 49)

Twisted ribbon rose (page 52)

Twisted chain stitch (page 52)

Whipstitch (page 53)

Outline Stitches

—·—·— Heavy chain stitch (page 43)

------ Stem stitch (page 51)

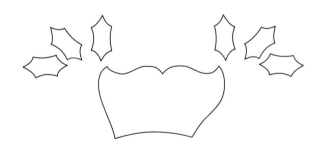

Appliqué Pieces

BLOCK 22

COLOR PHOTO ON PAGE 36.

Add a cutwork section to the urn, following the directions given for Block 6 (page 63).

To make the fishbone flower, gradually increase the stitch length as you work each set of petals.

Stitches

 Beads

 Bullion-tipped daisy (page 42)

 Colonial knots (page 43)

 Fishbone stitch (page 44)

French knot (page 45)

Lazy daisy (page 46)

 Loop stitch (page 47)

 Pinwheel flower (page 48)

 Ribbon stitch (page 49)

 Twisted ribbon flower (page 53)

Outline Stitches

 — ⋅ — ⋅ — Heavy chain stitch (page 43)

- - - - - Stem stitch (page 51)

Placement and Embroidery Guide

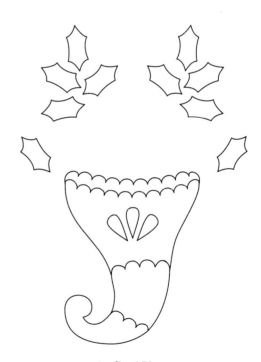

Appliqué Pieces

BLOCK 23

COLOR PHOTO ON PAGE 36.

Leave an opening in the center of the twisted chain stitch petals; make a small cluster of loop stitches in the center of the flower.

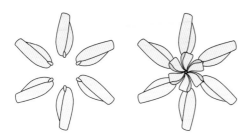

Stitches

 Colonial knots (page 43)

 Loop stitch (page 47)

Ribbon stitch (page 49)

 Twisted chain stitch (page 52)

Outline Stitch

------ Stem stitch (page 51)

Placement and Embroidery Guide

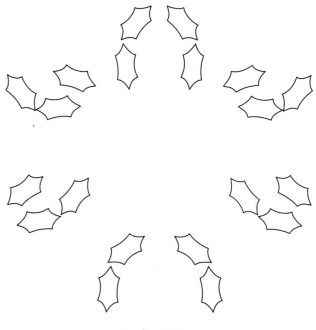

Appliqué Pieces

BLOCK 24

COLOR PHOTO ON PAGE 37.

Stitches

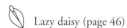 Colonial knots (page 43)

French knot (page 45)

Lazy daisy (page 46)

Ribbon stitch (page 49)

Twisted chain stitch (page 52)

Outline Stitch

- - - - - Stem stitch (page 51)

Placement and Embroidery Guide

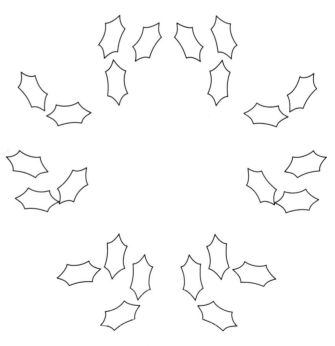

Appliqué Pieces

BLOCK 25

COLOR PHOTO ON PAGE 37.

This block may seem too dark, what with all those berries around the wreath. If you think so, substitute twisted-ribbon buds and ribbon-stitch leaves for some of the berries.

Stitches

 Colonial knots (page 43)

Coral stitch rose (page 43)

French knot (page 45)

Outline Stitch

- - - - - Stem stitch (page 51)

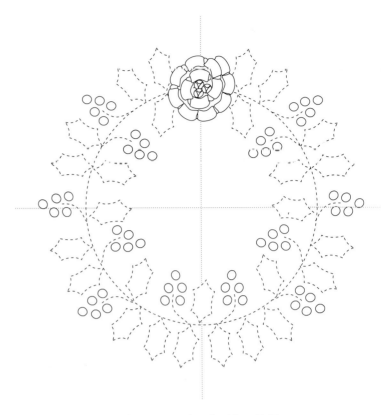

Placement and Embroidery Guide

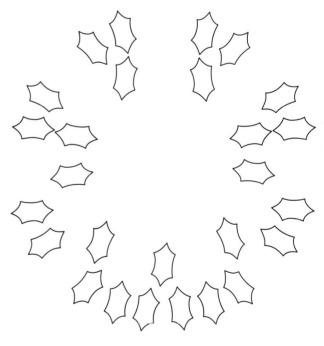

Appliqué Pieces

BLOCK 26

COLOR PHOTO ON PAGE 38.

Make a two-tone pinwheel flower, following the directions on page 48.

Stitches

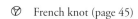 Colonial knots (page 43)

 French knot (page 45)

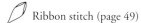 Pinwheel flower (page 48)

 Ribbon stitch (page 49)

Twisted chain stitch (page 52)

Outline Stitch

- - - - - Stem stitch (page 51)

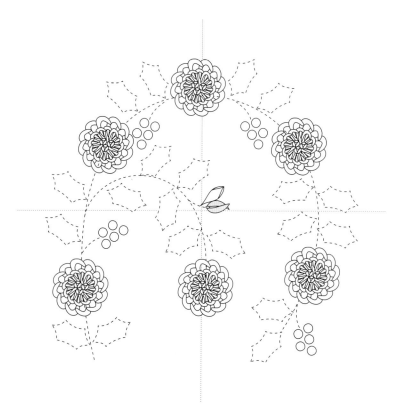

Placement and Embroidery Guide

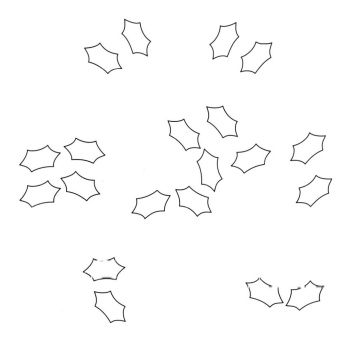

Appliqué Pieces

BLOCK 27

COLOR PHOTO ON PAGE 38.
Use two shades of ribbon for the whipstitches; alternate them as you work around the French-knot center.

Stitches

○○○ Colonial knots (page 43)

⊘ French knot (page 45)

◊ Ribbon stitch (page 49)

◊ Twisted chain stitch (page 52)

⬭ Whipstitch (page 53)

Outline Stitch

- - - - - Stem stitch (page 51)

Placement and Embroidery Guide

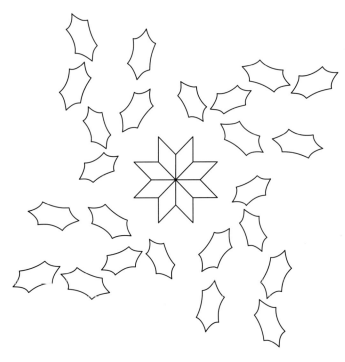

Appliqué Pieces

BLOCK 28

COLOR PHOTO ON PAGE 39.

For the flowers, make the twisted ribbon roses first. Thread a second shade of ribbon and surround each rose with a single row of stem stitches.

Stitches

 Colonial knots (page 43)

Stem stitch (ribbon) (page 51)

 Twisted ribbon rose (page 52)

Outline Stitch

- - - - - Stem stitch (page 51)

Placement and Embroidery Guide

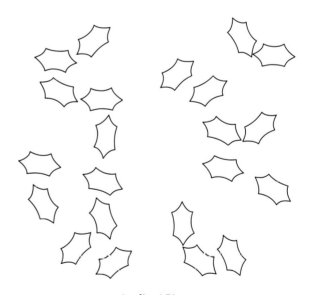

Appliqué Pieces

Block 29

COLOR PHOTO ON PAGE 39.

Stitches

 Colonial knots (page 43)

 French knot (page 45)

 Open loop stitch (page 48)

Ribbon stitch (page 49)

Twisted chain stitch (page 52)

Outline Stitch

 Stem stitch (page 51)

Placement and Embroidery Guide

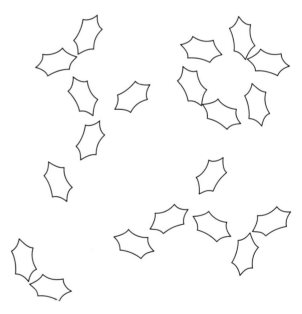

Appliqué Pieces

Block 30

COLOR PHOTO ON PAGE 40.

For the whipped backstitch flower, embroider a backstitch spiral, working out from the center. Whipstitch loosely over the backstitches in a second shade of ribbon. Add a French knot to the center to finish the flower.

Stitches

 Colonial knots (page 43)

 French knot (page 45)

 Ribbon stitch (page 49)

 Twisted chain stitch (page 52)

 Whipped backstitch (page 53)

Outline Stitch

- - - - - Stem stitch (page 51)

Placement and Embroidery Guide

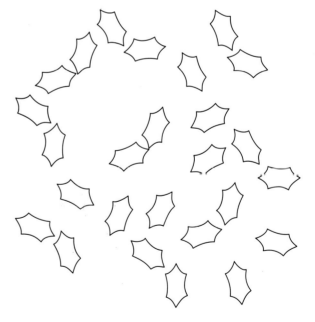

Appliqué Pieces

BLOCK 31

COLOR PHOTO ON PAGE 40.

Stitches

Colonial knots (page 43)

French knot (page 45)

Rosette chain flower (page 49)

Outline Stitch

- - - - - Stem stitch (page 51)

Placement and Embroidery Guide

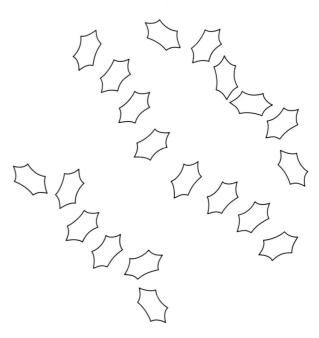

Appliqué Pieces

BLOCK 32

COLOR PHOTO ON PAGE 40.

Stitches

Colonial knots (page 43)

French knot (page 45)

Pistil stitch (page 49)

Ribbon stitch (page 49)

Twisted chain stitch (page 52)

Outline Stitch

- - - - - Stem stitch (page 51)

Placement and Embroidery Guide

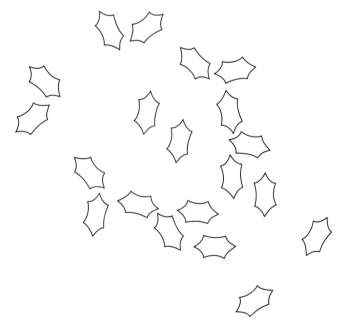

Appliqué Pieces

ASSEMBLING AND FINISHING YOUR QUILT

Blocking

If you did not use a hoop while embroidering, your finished blocks may be slightly puckered. It's common in patchwork to press blocks with an iron before assembling the quilt top. However, due to the silk-ribbon embroidery, these blocks cannot be pressed. Blocking—gently washing and stretching each block—eliminates puckers and ensures that your measurements are accurate when you assemble the quilt top. And since you probably will not want to wash the quilt after it is complete, now is a good time to clean and realign the blocks.

Many of my students are concerned about color-fastness, but if you have tested your fabrics, floss, thread, and ribbons you shouldn't have a problem.

You will need a dishpan, a sink, liquid dish soap, a terry cloth towel, straight pins, and a mounting board. A hair dryer also comes in handy. (Blow-drying perks up the damp ribbon, making it look like new.)

My mounting board is a 12" x 12" piece of cork glued to a plywood square. You can make a mounting board, or you can use a cork bulletin board, ceiling tile, or even the carpet in your living room. Any surface will work as long as it is clean, will not be damaged by the wet fabric, and can be stuck with pins. If using a mounting board, mark a grid so you can make sure the block is square.

1. Fill the dishpan with lukewarm water and a tiny bit of liquid dish soap. Gently swish a block around in the soapy water, then rinse thoroughly under cool, running tap water.

2. Using a folded terry cloth towel, gently pat (don't wring) the block to remove excess water.

3. Lay the block face up, pin the 4 corners, and place 3 to 4 pins along each side, stretching the block flat as you pin. Keep the block as square as possible.

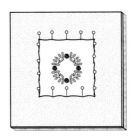

4. Allow the block to air-dry, or use a hair dryer.

NOTE

If you have used a material that could possibly bleed, and you do not wish to wash the blocks, you still have a blocking option. Fill a spray bottle with cool water and spritz the block on the back until just damp (not soaking). Follow the steps 2–4 of the blocking instructions. Blow-dry the block to get rid of the moisture as quickly as possible.

❋ ❋ ❋

Squaring the Blocks

It's time to trim your blocks to finished size. This is your last chance to make sure the design is centered. *Important*: Refer to "Choosing a Setting" on pages 5–7 for the finished size of your particular quilt blocks. Also, if you have opted for sashing between the blocks, refer to "Adding Sashing Strips" (below right) to determine the cut size.

You will need a piece of cardboard or template plastic; a ruler; a marking pencil; and craft scissors, fabric scissors, or rotary-cutting equipment.

1. Make a window template by marking and cutting a 4" or 5" square from the middle of the cardboard or template plastic. The size of the window is the finished size of the block, so for the straight setting (and for other design options in this book) the window size should be 4". Check your quilt design to make sure of your block size before you cut.
2. Place a block right side up. Center the design in the template window and mark a dot in each corner of the block. (You are marking the finished block size here, not the cutting lines.)
3. Remove the window template. Using a ruler and a marking pencil, draw a line ¼" from each side of the square formed by the marked dots. This is your cutting line.

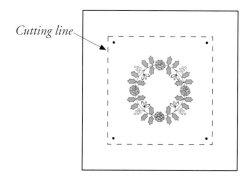

Cutting line

4. Using fabric scissors or rotary-cutting equipment, trim the blocks on the marked lines.

Assembling Straight Settings and Framed Blocks

Lay the blocks on a table, making sure your layout is pleasing and well-balanced. Sew the blocks together by hand or machine. If your blocks are diagonally set or sashed, see "Assembling Diagonal Settings" on pages 95–96 or "Adding Sashing Strips" below for special instructions. If you are setting the blocks straight without sashing, follow these steps:

1. Stitch the blocks together in horizontal rows, using a ¼" seam allowance. (Or lightly mark sewing lines ¼" from the block edges and stitch on these lines when joining the blocks.)
2. Gently press the seam allowances for each row in the same direction, alternating the direction from row to row. Don't smash the embroidery!
3. Stitch the horizontal rows together, butting the seam allowances between the blocks.

ADDING SASHING STRIPS

It can be a challenge to add sashing to a miniature quilt. Any misalignment will be magnified because of the small scale. If you do want sashing, you will need to lengthen the borders to fit your quilt. Instructions for lengthening border patterns are provided on page 97.

Pieced Sashing

1. Referring to "Squaring the Blocks" (at right), trim your blocks to 4½" x 4½".
2. Cut twelve ⅞"-wide fabric strips the width of the fabric. Cut those strips to the lengths and quantities needed for your quilt.

You will need at least ⅜ yard of fabric. This is enough to cut 12 strips, which should be adequate. For instance, if you were to make a sashed version of the Christmas quilt I used as an example in "Estimating Yardage and Cutting Blocks" on pages 7–8, you would need four 33"-long strips for the inner border, four 29" long strips for horizontal sashing, four 8½" strips, and twenty-four 4½" strips. *Warning*: Cut the longest strips first! Then cut strip lengths in decreasing order, to ensure that you'll have enough fabric.

3. Beginning ½" from the top of the strip, sew a sashing strip to the right side of the first block. Trim the strip so it is ½" longer than the block. Stitch the second block to the sashing strip, taking care to line it up with the first block. Trim the strip even with the blocks.

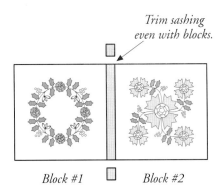

Trim sashing even with blocks.

Block #1   *Block #2*

4. Continue adding sashing strips between the blocks. Do not add a strip to the right side of the last block in each row.

5. Gently press the seam allowances for each row in the same direction, alternating the direction from row to row.

6. Sew a sashing strip to the top (top inner border) and bottom (sashing) of the first row. Trim the strips even with the blocks. Continue adding rows of blocks and strips, trimming the sashing strips as you go. Add a final sashing strip for the bottom inner border.

7. Sew sashing strips to the left and right sides of the quilt top (side inner borders). Trim the strips even with the blocks.

Appliquéd Sashing

1. Refer to "Squaring the Blocks" on page 93. Trim your blocks to 5½" x 5½".

2. Stitch the blocks together in horizontal rows. Gently press the seam allowances for each row in the same direction, alternating the direction from row to row.

3. Stitch the rows together, butting seam allowances.

4. You will need 1¼ yards of fabric to cut the strips. Cut 1½" x 45" strips of sashing fabric *lengthwise* along the straight of grain. For any of the projects suggested in this book, you could use up to 12 strips.

5. Fold the strips in half lengthwise, then in half again, with the raw edges slightly inside the second fold. Press the strips. (Hint: A quick squirt of spray starch while ironing will help give you crisp folds.) Baste the center of each strip to hold it together.

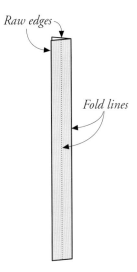

Raw edges

Fold lines

Fold strip in half, then in half again.

6. Center each basted sashing strip, raw edges down, on the seam lines. Appliqué the folded edges in place. (For instructions on appliqué, see "Appendix C" on page 109.)

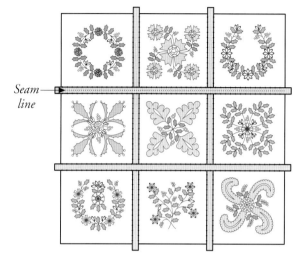

Seam line

NOTE
Appliqué the sashing strips to the outer edges of the quilt blocks after you add the borders.

❋   ❋   ❋

Assembling Diagonal Settings

I have suggested that you cut blocks on the straight of grain, then turn them on the bias for assembly. This would be a big problem for a larger quilt. The bias of cotton fabric has a slight stretch to it, which could work havoc along the edges of a quilt. Because you're making a miniature, however, you don't have to worry much about bias stretch. Just compensate for the bias problem by placing setting triangles so the long sides, which face the border, are on the straight of grain.

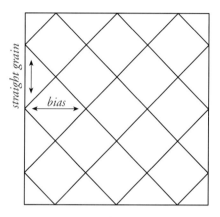

straight grain

bias

QUARTER-SQUARE TRIANGLES

You need a quarter-square triangle for each of the large setting triangles around the edge of the quilt. The long sides of these triangles finish on the straight of grain.

1. Trim each block to its finished size, adding a ¼" seam allowance.

2. Measure a block from corner to corner, not including seam allowances. This measurement is equal to the long sides of the setting triangles. For example, the diagonal measurement of a 4" finished-size block would be 5⁷⁄₁₆".

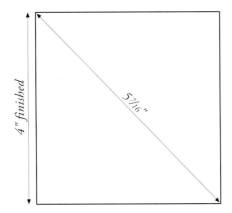

Add 1 ¼" to the diagonal measurement. For a 4" block: 5⁷⁄₁₆" + 1¼" = 6¹¹⁄₁₆". Cut squares to the measurement you determined.

3. Stack the squares and cut them twice diagonally, yielding 4 triangles per square.

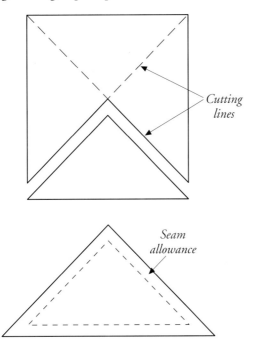

Cutting lines

Seam allowance

HALF-SQUARE TRIANGLES

You need two squares to cut four triangles for the corners of the quilt. The short sides of these triangles finish on the straight of grain.

1. Add ⅞" to the finished size of your block, for seam allowances. For example, the measurement for a 4" finished-size block would be 4⅞". Cut 2 squares to the measurement you determined.

2. Stack the squares and cut them once diagonally, yielding 2 triangles per square.

Assembling the Quilt Top

1. Lay out the blocks in diagonal rows. Stitch the rows together, including the setting triangles.

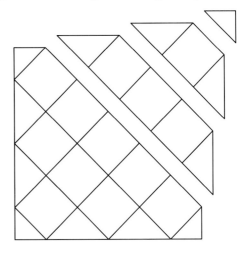

2. Gently press the seam allowances for each row in the same direction, alternating the direction from row to row. Be careful not to press the embroidery.

3. Stitch the rows together, butting seam allowances.

4. Add borders, if desired.

Adding Borders

The border is the finishing touch on any quilt. This book includes two border variations, along with adaptations for the framed blocks. The embroidery in the borders coordinate with the medallion block. Feel free to adapt your silk-ribbon flowers to complement choices you've made for your quilt.

Before you cut or mark your fabrics, make a full-size pattern for one side of your quilt. This will make it easier to estimate border size and to transfer the design to the fabric.

When tracing appliqué patterns, remember to draw on the paper side of the fusible web.

BORDERS FOR STRAIGHT SETTINGS WITHOUT SASHING

Use this method for straight-set blocks without sashing and for framed blocks.

1. To calculate the length of the border for one side, multiply the number of blocks by 4.
2. Cut a piece of freezer paper 8" longer than the length calculated in step 1. (Add 12" for the framed-blocks setting.) Using a pencil, draw a straight line along one long side, as shown.
3. Working from the left side, align the corner pattern with the pencil line and trace the border design onto the freezer paper.

4. Continue tracing border sections, repeating as needed to allow for the number of blocks across your quilt.
5. Trace a second corner at the other end.

BORDERS FOR QUILTS WITH SASHING OR DIAGONAL SETTINGS

1. Measure the width of your quilt top across the center. Subtract ½" for outside seam allowances.
2. Cut a piece of freezer paper 8" longer than the length calculated in step 1. Using a pencil, draw a straight line along one long side, the same length as calculated in step 1. Mark the center of the pencil line, as shown.
3. On separate pieces of paper, trace the sections you need, based on the number of blocks across your quilt. Do not include corners. Cut the sections along the center lines.
4. Using the center mark on the freezer paper as a guide, lay the cut sections along the length of the pencil line. Tape the sections to the freezer paper.
5. Cut a piece of freezer paper the same length as in step 2. Lay this piece on the border pattern and trace. Fill the gaps with stems, leaves, or flowers.
6. Add the corner sections to the ends.

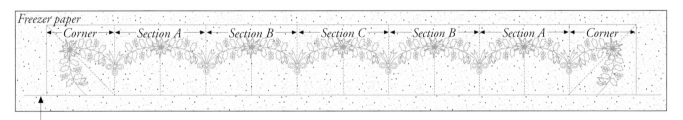

Pencil line

Border without Sashing

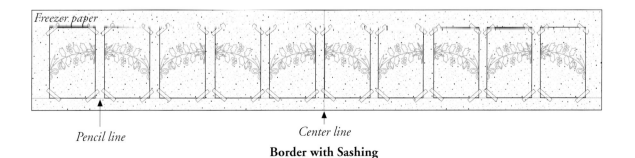

Pencil line

Center line

Border with Sashing

CONSTRUCTING BORDERS WITHOUT FRAMES

To make borders without frames, you will need: border and appliqué fabric, paper-backed fusible web, a pencil or permanent-ink black marker, a marking pencil, an iron and ironing surface, and small embroidery scissors.

1. Using your freezer-paper pattern as a guide, cut 4 strips of border fabric approximately 1" larger than needed all around. Add ¼"-wide seam allowances around the border pattern.

2. Center 1 border strip over the pattern. Using a marking pencil, trace the design, including corners, on the fabric. Mark the outside edges so you can add seam allowances; you can trim excess fabric later. Repeat with another border strip.

3. Center and trace the pattern on the remaining 2 strips, omitting the corner sections.

4. Using a pencil, trace all the appliqué pieces for 1 border strip on the paper side of the fusible web.

5. Cut the appliqué pieces apart. Referring to the manufacturer's instructions, fuse a section to the wrong side of the appliqué fabric. Repeat for each group of appliqué pieces.

6. Using small embroidery scissors, cut out the appliqué pieces.

7. Working as gently as possible, peel the paper backing from the appliqués.

8. Fuse the appliqués to the border strips, following the pattern lines.

9. Trim each border strip to fit the quilt top. (Remember to add seam allowances to all 4 sides of the border strip before cutting to fit.)

10. Sew the borders without corner sections to the quilt top first, then add the borders with corner sections. Make sure the corners match up with the ends of the borders already attached.

11. Embroider as desired.

CONSTRUCTING FRAMED BORDERS

You need: background and frame fabric(s), appliqué fabrics, paper-backed fusible web, a pencil, marking pencil, an iron and ironing surface, and small embroidery scissors.

Plan where you want the seams for each border section to end. For more stability and visual appeal, do not align the background and framing seams. Plan for a mitered seam on either the background or the frame fabric.

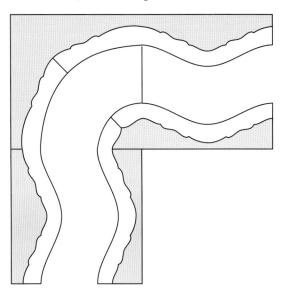

Note
It is easiest to mark the design for both background and frames onto rectangular strips of fabric. You can trim the excess fabric when you appliqué the sections together. Remember to allow ample space for seam allowances on all four sides of each section.

※   ※   ※

1. Using your freezer-paper pattern as a guide, cut 4 strips of background fabric approximately 1" larger than needed all around.

2. Center one of the background strips over the pattern. Trace both the frame line and the embroidery pattern. Repeat for a second strip.

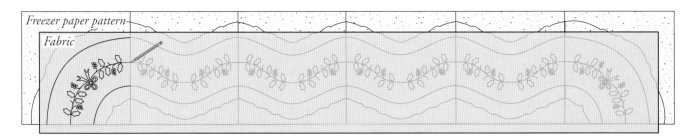

Freezer paper pattern

Fabric

3. Center and trace the remaining two strips, omitting the corner sections.

4. From the frame fabric, cut 4 strips, each 1" larger than the inner frame, and 4 more strips, each 1" larger than the outer frame. Trace the frame lines onto your fabrics. If you have planned mitered corners for this frame, mark all 4 sections the same.

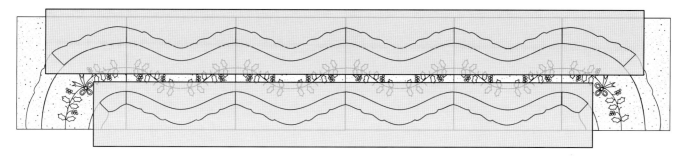

5. If you are making a double-frame border, cut and mark those strips as you did the previous ones.

6. Referring to steps 4–8 of "Constructing Borders without Frames" on page 00, prepare the appliqué pieces and fuse them to the background fabric.

7. Trim each piece of the inner frame border to size, leaving a ¼" seam allowance. Attach the 4 sections to the body of the quilt, then stitch the corner seams. Set the quilt top aside.

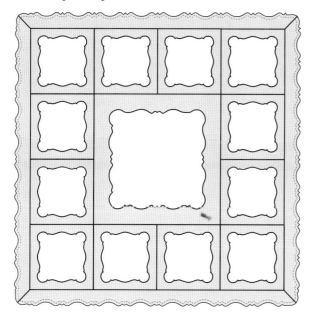

8. Trim the 2 short sides of each background strip, leaving a ¼" seam allowance. Sew the 4 sections together, matching the corner seams.

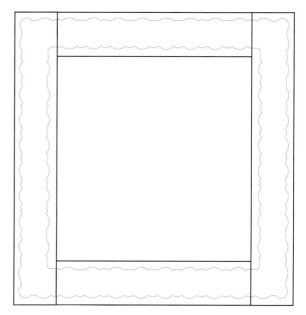

9. Trim the corners of each outer frame section, leaving a ¼" seam allowance. Sew the 4 sections together. (This would be the middle section if you are making a double border.) Trim only the inside of the frame, including a ¼" seam allowance.

10. Lay the background border on a table and arrange the outer frame border on top, aligning the marked appliqué lines. Baste the borders together.

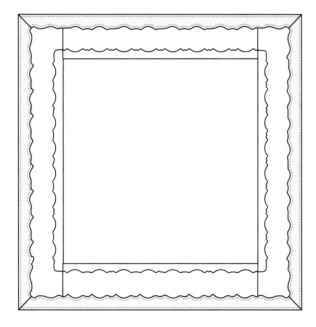

Appliqué the background border and outer frame border together, using matching thread and following the marked lines. When you are finished, turn the border over and carefully trim the excess background fabric from the appliqué, leaving a scant ¼" seam allowance. (If you are making a double-frame border, repeat this step with the inner middle frame and the outermost frame, trimming the excess fabric behind each and leaving a small seam allowance.)

11. Lay the assembled border on a table. Arrange the quilt on top, aligning the marked appliqué lines. Baste the two together.

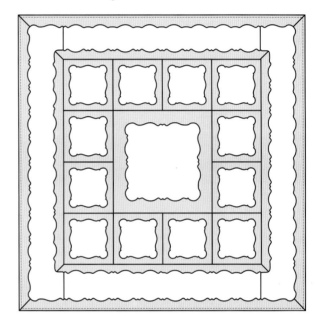

Appliqué the quilt to the border, using matching thread. Trim the excess fabric from behind, leaving a small seam allowance.

12. Embroider the stems, leaves, and flowers onto the border background.

Marking Quilting Designs

When choosing a quilting design, keep in mind that you will not want to quilt through the embroidered block designs; the fused fabrics tend to gum up your needle and are difficult to penetrate.

Use the marker of your choice to mark your quilting design. I prefer chalk marking pencils. They usually wear off, and if they don't, you can spritz them away with water. *Test your marking pencil before you begin. Always mark lightly.*

Layering and Basting

I like to use the same fabric for my quilt top and backing. Whatever you decide, be sure to choose a good quality fabric for the backing. Remember that dark backing fabric may shadow through the front of a light quilt top. Choose an easy-to-quilt, low-loft batting.

1. Cut the backing fabric and batting 4" larger all around than the size of your quilt.
2. Lay the backing on a table or carpet, wrong side up. Using masking tape, fasten the backing to your working surface. Make sure there aren't any puckers or folds in the fabric, but do not stretch the fabric out of shape.
3. Smooth the batting on top of the backing.
4. Lay the quilt top, right side up, on the batting, making sure the fabric grain is placed the same for the top and backing. Tape the corners of the quilt top to the work surface.
5. Beginning in the center, baste the layers. Work diagonally from corner to corner, then in a 4" grid across the quilt.

Quilting

Some people have no problem quilting without a hoop, but I can't seem to keep my stitches neat and even unless I use one. Since a hoop tends to crush silk-ribbon embroidery, I solved the problem by adapting a set of artist's stretcher bars, available at craft and art-supply stores. Purchase a set approximately the same size as your quilt top. (Make sure, before you buy the bars, that you will be able to comfortably reach the quilt center while the quilt is in the frame.) You will also need twelve large binder clips—the sort used to hold papers together—which are available at office-supply stores.

Assemble the stretcher bars into a square frame, then lay the basted quilt over the frame. Using the binder clips, clamp the quilt to the frame. As you work, move the binder clips out of your way. This method also works well for larger quilts, especially those with delicate dimensional appliqué.

You will also need: quilting thread, needles (Betweens), and a thimble. Use the smallest needle you are comfortable with.

1. Cut an 18"-long piece of quilting thread. Thread the needle with a single strand of thread and make a small knot at one end. Insert the needle in the top layer of the quilt, a slight distance from where you want to start stitching, then pull it out where you want to begin. Gently tug on the thread until the knot pops through the fabric and buries itself in the batting.
2. Using a running stitch, take small, even stitches through all 3 layers of the quilt, as shown. Rock the needle up and down, placing 3 to 4 stitches on your needle at once. Place your other hand under the quilt so you can feel the needle point with each stitch.

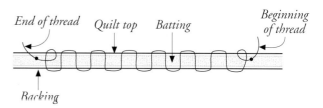

3. To end a row of quilting, make a small knot next to the last stitch. Backstitch through the layers, about a needle's length away, and gently pull on the thread to pop the knot into the batting. Carefully trim the thread end even with the quilt top.

Adding a Hanging Sleeve

Unless you decide to frame your finished quilt, you will want to attach a sleeve for hanging.

1. Cut a 6" to 8"-wide strip of fabric that is 1" shorter than the width of the quilt. Turn the short ends under ½" twice and stitch.

2. Fold the strip in half lengthwise, wrong sides together, and baste the raw edges to the quilt back, aligning them with the top edge. Don't worry about this raw edge; it will be finished when the binding is attached to your quilt.

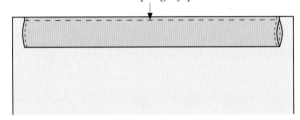

Baste sleeve to top edge of quilt back.

3. After attaching the binding (see below), blindstitch the bottom of the sleeve to the quilt. Push the bottom of the sleeve up slightly before stitching; this provides a little "give" so the hanging rod does not put strain on the quilt.

Binding

French double-fold binding is durable, attractive, and can be made from bias or straight-grain fabric strips.

1. Measure around the perimeter of the quilt, add 10" for seams and mitered corners, then cut enough 2½"-wide strips of fabric to bind the quilt. For example, if your quilt is 27" x 27", you would need 118" of binding strips.

    If you cut your strips from straight-grain fabric, ½ yard should be enough for any quilt design in this book. If you cut bias strips, you'll need approximately ¾ yard.

2. Join the binding strips right sides together, as shown, to make one long piece of binding. Press the seams open.

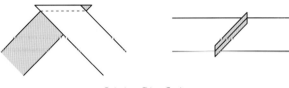

Joining Bias Strips

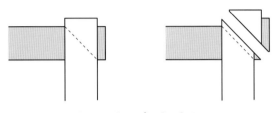

Joining Straight-Cut Strips

3. Fold the binding in half lengthwise, wrong sides together, and press.

4. Turn under one end of the strip at a 45° angle and press. This eliminates bulk where the ends meet.

5. Trim the batting and backing even with the quilt top.

6. Using a ⅜"-wide seam allowance, stitch the binding to the front of the quilt, aligning the raw edges of the binding and quilt. At the corners, stop and backstitch ⅜" from the edge, as shown. Trim the thread.

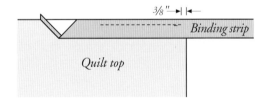

7. Rotate the quilt 90° and align the binding and quilt top edges so you can stitch down the next side. Fold the binding up and away from the quilt at a 45° angle.

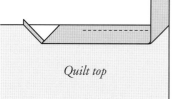

Quilt top

8. Fold the binding back onto itself, parallel with the edge of the quilt, to finish mitering the corner. Start stitching again, ⅜" from the corner, backstitching at the edge.

⅜"

Quilt top

9. Continue stitching around the quilt, mitering corners as you come to them. When you reach the beginning of the binding, overlap the ends about 1". Trim at a 45° angle. Tuck the raw end into the fold and finish the seam.

Quilt top

10. Fold the binding to the back of the quilt, covering the seam, and blindstitch in place. Miter and blindstitch the corners as you go.

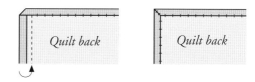

Quilt back   *Quilt back*

Signing Your Quilt

Be sure to sign and date your quilt, either on the back or in one of the front blocks. Include as much information as possible: your name, the name of the quilt, dates you worked on the quilt, and your location. If you are making a label for the back, include the recipient's name, if a gift, or other information about the making of the quilt.

APPENDIXES

Appendix A:
Frame Patterns

SINGLE FRAME MEDALLION

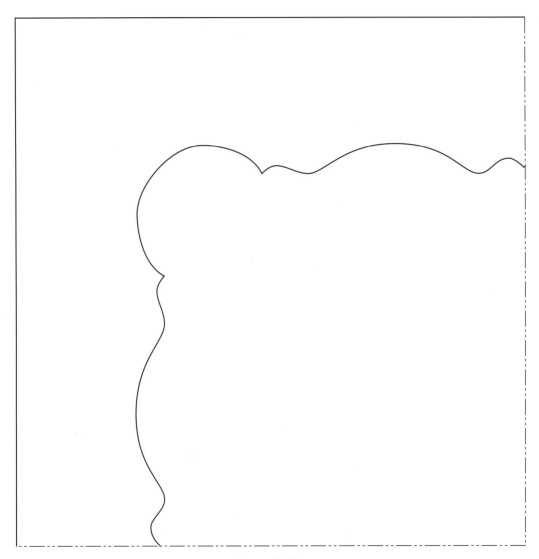

Corner Section
Trace 4, flipping as needed, for full medallion.

DOUBLE FRAME MEDALLION

Corner Section
Trace 4, flipping as needed, for full medallion.

SINGLE FRAME BLOCK

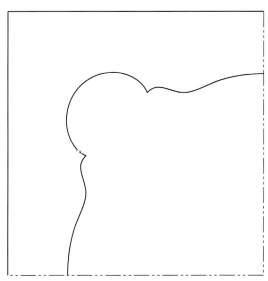

Corner Section
Trace 4, flipping as needed, for full block.

DOUBLE FRAME BLOCK

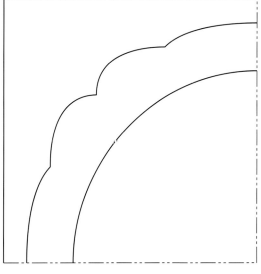

Corner Section
Trace 4, flipping as needed, for full block.

Appendix B: Border Patterns

BORDER 1

Corner Section

BORDER 2

Corner Section

Swag Section

Swag Section

SINGLE FRAME BORDER

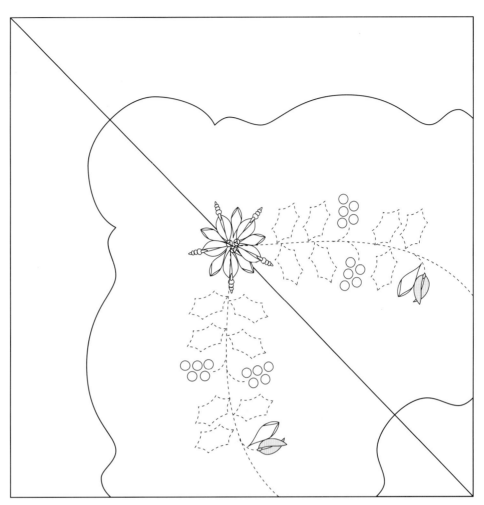

Corner Section

SINGLE FRAME BORDER

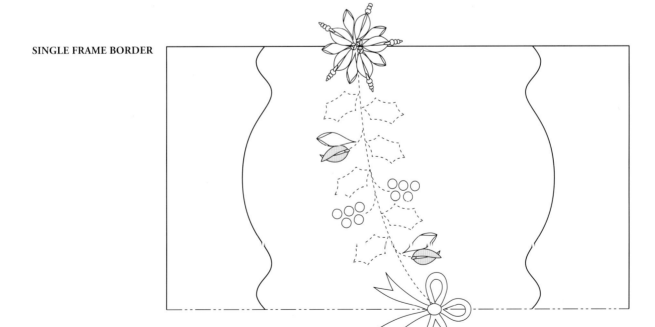

Half Swag Section
Trace, then flip and trace again for full section.

Corner Section

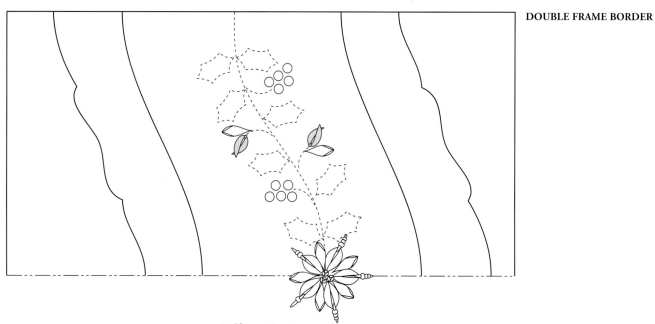

Half Swag Section
Trace, then flip and trace again for full section

Appendix C: Needleturn Appliqué

Needleturn appliqué is simply using your needle to turn under the seam allowance for a short distance, then using an appliqué or blind stitch to sew the appliqué in place. The framed blocks and borders in this book are easily stitched in place with this method.

1. Mark the appliqué design on your fabric, then cut it out, adding a scant ¼" seam allowance.

2. Position the appliqué on the background fabric and pin or baste it in place.

3. Thread an appliqué needle (Sharp) with about 18" of thread that matches the appliqué piece. Knot one end of the thread.

4. Begin at a relatively straight area of the appliqué. Work from right to left if you are right-handed, and from left to right if you are left-handed. Bring the needle through the quilt top and use the tip of the needle to gently turn under a ½" length of the seam allowance. Hold this "basted" area with the thumb and first finger of your other hand.

5. Bring the needle through the edge of the appliqué, catching only a thread or two. Move the needle directly off the appliqué and through the background fabric. Without pulling the needle all the way through, ride the needle under the background fabric, parallel to the edge of the appliqué, then bring it back up under the appliqué, about ⅛" away. Catch only a thread or two of the appliqué fabric, then give the thread a slight tug and continue to stitch along the ½" you turned under.

6. When the section is finished, use your needle to turn under another ½". Keep stitching until finished, then fasten the thread on the back.

HINT

Clip sparingly along inside curves to make turning under the seam allowance easier.

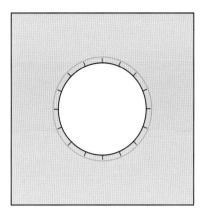

Clip curves.

✳   ✳   ✳

NOTE

For outside corners, stitch up to the corner and take your last stitch in the tip. Turn under the other side, folding twice as shown.

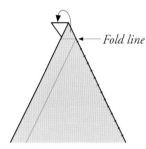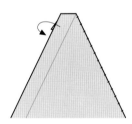

← Fold line

First fold brings corner to meet appliquéd side.

Second fold continues on marked line.

✳   ✳   ✳

RESOURCES

HAND-DYED SILK RIBBON
Jenifer Buechel
Box 118
3567 Mountainview Drive
West Mifflin, PA 15122
jbuechel@pgh.net
*Eighty-four variegated shades of silk ribbon
are available in a variety of widths, as well as
braids. Send $2 for a color card
and ordering information.*

SEWING ACCESSORIES
Clotilde, Inc.
Highway 54 West
Louisiana, MO 63353
1-800-772-2891
*Call for a free catalog. Clotilde carries
everything from needles and scissors
to ribbons and threads.*

FLOSS AND THREADS
Bernadine's Needle Art Catalog
PO Box 41
Department BA
Arthur, IL 61911
Send $2 for a catalog.

BIBLIOGRAPHY

EMBROIDERY AND APPLIQUÉ
Heazlewood, Merrilyn. *One Hundred Embroidery Stitches.* New York: Coats and Clark, 1964.

Kimball, Jeanna. *Red and Green: An Appliqué Tradition.* Bothell, Wash.: That Patchwork Place, Inc., 1990.

Kolter, Jane Bentley. *Forget Me Not.* Pittstown, New Jersey: The Main Street Press, 1985.

Montano, Judith Baker. *The Art of Silk Ribbon Embroidery.* Lafayette, Calif.: C & T Publishing, 1993.

Nichols, Marion. *Encyclopedia of Embroidery Stitches Including Crewel.* New York: Dover Publications, Inc., 1974.

Sienkiewicz, Elly. *Baltimore Album Quilts: Historic Notes and Antique Patterns; A Pattern Companion to Baltimore Beauties and Beyond, Vol. 1.* Lafayette, Calif.: C & T Publishing, 1990.

Sienkiewicz, Elly. *Baltimore Beauties and Beyond: Studies in Classic Album Quilt Appliqué, Volume 2.* Lafayette, Calif.: C & T Publishing, 1991.

QUILTING
Hanson, Joan, and Mary Hickey. *The Joy of Quilting.* Bothell, Wash.: That Patchwork Place, Inc., 1994.

MEET THE AUTHOR

Born and raised in Pittsburgh, Pennsylvania, Jenifer Buechel has a full house with her husband, Ron; two teenagers, Heather and Ryan; two old dogs; and two young cats. She has been quilting for approximately fourteen years, and has tried more crafts, sewing, and needle-arts projects than she can remember. After winning several quilting awards, she began teaching at a local quilt shop. Since then, she's been designing original quilts and class projects.

This is her second That Patchwork Place book. Her first, Miniature Baltimore Album Quilts, *was published in 1997.*

INDEX OF STITCHES